CONTENTS

Ships in Focus Publications

Correspondence and editorial:
Roy Fenton
18 Durrington Avenue
London SW20 8NT
020 8879 3527
record@rfenton.co.uk

Orders and photographic:
John & Marion Clarkson
18 Franklands, Longton
Preston PR4 5PD
01772 612855
shipsinfocus@btinternet.com

© 2013 Individual contributors,
John Clarkson and Roy Fenton.

Printed by Amadeus Press Ltd.,
Cleckheaton, Yorkshire.
Designed by Hugh Smallwood, John Clarkson and Roy Fenton.

SHIPS IN FOCUS RECORD
ISBN 978-1-901703-25-2

SUBSCRIPTION RATES FOR RECORD

Readers can start their subscription with any issue, and are welcome to backdate it to receive previous issues.

	3 issues	4 issues
UK	£24	£31
Europe (airmail)	£26	£34
Rest of the world (surface mail)	£26	£34
Rest of the world (airmail)	£31	£41

SHIPS IN FOCUS

March 2013

The ghost of a much-missed contributor visits this issue of 'Record'. By courtesy of Wenslie Naylon, we are delighted to run the first part of John Naylon's article on French bounty ships, which was unfinished on his untimely death in 2010. The manuscript required only the gentlest of editing, but John had not started the captions for the photographs which he had chosen, and the editors hope that they have placed them appropriately to illustrate the points he makes in the text.

This is an appropriate point to make our annual invitation to potential contributors. Until fairly recently in the history of 'Record', we were pleased to find that each issue had an article by someone who had not contributed before. As time went on this inevitably diminished, but we remain very welcoming to contributors new or established. As to subject matter, we are open to histories of shipping companies, shipbuilders, ship breakers, types and classes of ship, aspects of naval architecture, marine engineering, the merchant navy at war, ports and harbours, and books about ships and shipping. Although the editors' preference for 'classic' cargo ships is well-known, this should not be a limiting factor, and coverage of tugs, trawlers, tankers and other breeds are particularly welcome as types that we have tended to neglect.

We would simply ask that any submission has an element of original research and that it can be illustrated photographically. Themed photographic features are also very acceptable, and we would encourage the writing up of well-known ship photographers (although to avoid accusations of favouritism, a condition is that the photographer is dead!). Fleet lists are not obligatory, and in fact we try to limit the number in each 'Record' (although with two and a bit, we have failed to do so in this issue). We are also happy to give assistance with research and photo searches, although we usually expect the author to do a significant amount of both themselves.

Our usual policy is to have enough material for at least two issues on hand, so once a submission has been accepted it is likely to appear within 12 months. As always, contributors are earnestly advised to give us notice of anything they intend to work up. This not only avoids disappointment if we decide their theme does not match our editorial policy, but it also means we may be able to advise on sources. A style sheet is available from what we describe as our 'London office', to which any enquiries about submissions should be directed.

Apologies to those awaiting a continuation of 'South West Scenes'; part 2 has been held over until 'Record' 55.

John Clarkson   Roy Fenton

Her pristine hull suggests the ill-fated *Swanley* has just been completed. See page 74 onwards. *[Glasgow University Archives UGD136/2/1/40]*

Although the financial interests of the Lambtons in the collieries and ships had long since gone, the Tanfield company still retained the traditional 'three red bands' funnel marking of the family, and *Harraton* of 1930 carried the name of a colliery village adjacent to their main residence, Lambton Castle. In February 1939 she was sold to Société Anonyme 'Le Nickel', Le Havre, France who renamed her *Cagou* and used her in conjunction with their nickel mining activities on Pacific islands. On 23rd July 1942 she sailed from Sydney during a voyage from Port Kembla to Nouméa and disappeared. She is believed to have been sunk by the Japanese submarine *I-175* on 28th July 1942 north east of Sydney. *[Frank and Sons Ltd./ Author's collection]*

AUSTIN'S 'CHELWOOD' TYPE COLLIERS
The development of the 4,000dwt engines-aft design
John Lingwood

Marine photographers Frank and Sons Ltd. were ideally based at South Shields, just a few miles south from the Measured Mile course on the Northumberland Coast, to take photographs of new ships under way and undergoing acceptance trials, and several examples of their work are amongst the illustrations to this article. *Harraton* (left) illustrates the prototype 4,000-ton, engines-aft collier of the 1920s, whilst the photograph of *Sea Fisher* (below) shows not only how that design was modernised during the next decade, but how the vessel was adapted to carry out an important Second World War function.

As early as the seventeenth century, sailing ships ('collier brigs') are recorded as being used to transport coal from the Durham and Northumberland coalfields to satisfy the insatiable appetites of domestic and commercial users in London and the south of England, laying the foundations of what became generally known as the North East Coast coal trade. The mid-nineteenth century saw the introduction of the first steam colliers, built (since the propeller was there) with their propelling machinery at the after end of the ship. Subsequently this layout was used quite satisfactorily for coasters and small vessels of up to about 2,500 tons deadweight, but adoption of the arrangement for larger ships of around 4,000 tons deadweight had been

considered undesirable. The objections to the design were based mainly on perceived problems of trim in both loaded and ballast conditions, distribution of water ballast, and structural weakness, particularly when a raised quarter deck configuration with a consequent break in the continuous strength deck was used. As a result, the few colliers built to carry these larger deadweights usually had machinery amidships and, although some of these retained the raised quarter deck layout, the majority were single-decked with forecastle, poop and midship bridge erections; similar, in fact to the then typical design of the larger deep sea tramp.

The midship-engined design itself presented problems: these were mainly caused by the necessity to have a shaft tunnel running through the after holds. As these compartments narrowed towards the stern, access to tank top level for grab discharge became constricted, resulting in considerable damage to adjacent structures, particularly the tunnel top. In 1922 William France, Fenwick and Co. Ltd., one of the leading operators in the North East coal trade, placed orders for six, midship-engined, raised quarter deck colliers of sizes between 2,900 and 3,300 tons deadweight, deciding that a solution to the problems caused by the shaft tunnel was to raise the tank top in the after holds to the level of the tunnel top. Unfortunately, neither owner nor the

SEA FISHER

It is interesting to note that whilst most wartime new buildings were delivered in overall grey paint and without owners' identification, *Sea Fisher* of 1940 appears in this trials' photograph to have retained her 'peacetime' livery. The cross on the hull amidships indicates the ship has been over the degaussing range and her hull has been 'wiped' for protection against magnetic mines. *Sea Fisher* remained in the Fisher fleet until 1956 when she became *Malcolm* of the Shamrock Shipping Co. Ltd. of Belfast. After sale to the Great Ocean Steam Ship Co. Ltd. (An Kuo Steam Ship Co. Ltd.) of Taiwan in 1959, she was renamed *New Country*, and retained this name after management was transferred to the China Merchants Steam Navigation Company in 1966. Scrapping in 1967 soon followed. *[Frank and Sons Ltd./ Author's collection]*

shipbuilders involved had considered the effect on stability that taking away a substantial weight of cargo from the bottom of the ship would have, and the four larger units were extremely tender in the loaded condition, and had to have the modification removed from Number 3 hold at considerable expense, in order to remedy this unforeseen problem.

It was four years after this unfortunate experience before France, Fenwick again entered the newbuilding market. This time, under pressure from new and younger board members, the company decided to build to the machinery-aft design. Whereas the previous six vessels had been built by companies of the highest repute but with no great experience of collier building, this time the order was placed with S.P. Austin and Sons Ltd. of Sunderland, well established as builders of this type of vessel. A full and detailed specification was agreed between owner and builder in an attempt to overcome the previously held doubts surrounding 'large', raised quarter deck colliers with engines aft, and the new vessel was delivered in 1928 as *Chelwood* at a cost of £42,500. Her dimensions were 306 feet long; 43 feet 9 inches beam and 21 feet 6 inches depth, with a deadweight of 4,190 tons and gross tonnage 2,742.

The navigating bridge was positioned about midships at the break of the upper and raised quarter decks, and there were four cargo holds, two forward and two aft of the bridge, below which was a water ballast tank. Masts were stepped between numbers 1 and 2 and between 3 and 4 hatches with a single derrick serving each hatch, and the triple-expansion propelling machinery was supplied by the North Eastern Marine Engineering Co. Ltd., Sunderland.

That the *Chelwood* design was successful is evidenced by the fact that France, Fenwick quickly ordered a sister ship from Austins, taking delivery of *Chatwood* in 1929. A modification included in her construction demonstrated one of the many factors which had to be considered by owners when deciding to build new ships, in this case the type of cargo to be carried. The larger units in the France, Fenwick fleet at that time were generally employed carrying from the Humber to the near Continent cargoes of washed coal, a commodity which stowed badly and, as a consequence, holds were often full before the ships were down to their marks. Therefore, to increase capacity the hatch coamings in *Chatwood* were increased in height by nine inches and were built with sloping sides and ends. For

France, Fenwick's pioneering *Chelwood* of 1928 (above and right) steamed through the Second World War and gave the collier company an outstanding 29 years of service. Sale in 1957 saw her go east, to a subsidiary of Wheelock, Marden and Co. Ltd. of Hong Kong who put her under the Panama flag as *San Romeli*. The ageing collier did not survive long, however, as in January 1960 she was towed from Hong Kong to Kaohsiung for demolition. *[Both: Roy Fenton collection]*

Completed in June 1929, *Chatwood* was a development of *Chelwood* with increased capacity and could load almost four thousand tons of coal. When sunk after being mined near the East Dudgeon Buoy in the North Sea on 23rd April 1942 she had on board 3,950 tons of Tyne coal for the Thames. Fortunately her 24 crew and three gunners were saved. The photograph was taken on trials, undoubtedly by Frank and Sons Ltd. *[David Whiteside collection]*

cargoes of other grades of coal to the continent, customers' requirements were for shipments of around 3,000 tons, and with this in mind the next 'Chelwood' new building, *Bushwood* of 1930, was a smaller version with a deadweight of 3,540 tons.

In 1930 Austins booked their first order for a 'Chelwood' type collier from an owner other than France, Fenwick, and Frank and Sons' photograph of *Harraton* on page 66 illustrates the design. In fact, this vessel was that touch bigger all round than the prototype, with dimensions of 308 feet long x 44 feet 3 inches beam and 21 feet 9 inches depth, sufficient to give her a deadweight of 4,300 tons and a gross tonnage of 2,795. A service speed of nine knots on a consumption of 18 tons per day, derived from a North Eastern Marine triple-expansion engine, was deemed adequate by *Harraton's* owner, the Tanfield Steamship Co.

Next completion by Austin for France, Fenwick, the *Bushwood* of January 1930, had a length of 283 feet and a gross tonnage of 2,314, compared with 306 feet and 2,768 gross tons for her immediate predecessor *Chatwood*. *Bushwood* was requisitioned by the Royal Navy during the Second World War and commissioned first as a magnetic minesweeper, later as a degaussing vessel and finally as a stores vessel. Sale in 1947 saw her work in the Far East until Hong Kong breakers started to demolish her in March 1951. *[David Whiteside collection]*

Ltd. of Newcastle, a company registered in 1920 to take over what remained of the once extensive collier fleet set up by the Lambton Collieries combine (controlled by the Earls of Durham) nearly a century earlier to ship coal from the Durham coalfield. In 1896 the Lambton interests were acquired by local rival James Joicey (later the first Lord Joicey) and it was his family which subscribed most of the capital for the Tanfield company.

Frank's photographs show the rather austere appearance of the 1920s collier. Never owning more than

five ships, Tanfield's trading pattern became a mix of having perhaps a couple of vessels regularly employed serving Beckton Gas Works in the summer and three in the winter, with the others taking coal to the Continent and Mediterranean and returning with iron ore from Spain or North Africa to North East United Kingdom ports. Another summer trade was the import of timber (typically for use as pit props in the Lambton collieries) from Russian White Sea ports. *Harraton* was a regular trader to the French port of Rouen, so it was probably no surprise when she was sold to a French owner in February 1939 for £55,000 - showing a profit of £10,500 over her building cost.

Tanfield already had a replacement for *Harraton* lined up, and in December 1939 *Lea Grange* was completed for them by Austins. She was, in effect, the last of the pre-war, direct descendents of *Chelwood's* design, and a modern sister of *Harraton* with a deadweight of 4,500 tons and a speed of 10 knots.

During the 1930s France, Fenwick had continued to build a mix of 3,000 and 4,000 tons deadweight colliers with Austins, modifying the basic specification as developments

in ship and propelling machinery design had been introduced. *Dalewood* (1931) was the first vessel in the fleet to be fitted with superheaters (she was also the first collier on the coast to use superheated steam), and the propelling machinery installed by North Eastern Marine in *Goodwood* (1937) was of their new design incorporating a low pressure turbine *Wychwood* (1934) was the first France, Fenwick vessel to have a cruiser stern and *Hawkwood*, also delivered in 1934, is claimed to have been the collier which revolutionised coal discharge by having hoppered sides in the holds. However, it was not until 1942 that MacGregor steel hatch covers were

Harraton's replacement, *Lea Grange*, was delivered to the Tanfield Steamship Co. Ltd. in December 1939, remaining with this company until it was wound up about ten years later. She then passed with her slightly smaller Austin-built running mate *Lambtonian* of 1942 to Stephenson Clarke Ltd. The only change was the replacement of the three red bands on her black funnel (supposedly depicting the legendary Lambton worm, and barely discernible in the first photograph) with Stephenson Clarkes' silver band (second photo). *Lea Grange* was sold to Greece as *Costicos* in 1959 (third photo, taken in July 1970). Laid up in Piraeus since 1971, the Lebanese-flagged steamer arrived at Istanbul under tow in June 1973 and was broken up at Halic. *[Top and middle: Roy Fenton collection, bottom: J. and M. Clarkson]*

fitted by the company; if memory serves, the first installation of these to a collier was to a William Cory vessel just prior to the Second World War.

Frank and Sons' photograph of *Sea Fisher* on page 67 illustrates some of the changes made to the *Chelwood* design between 1930 and 1940. Completed in May 1940 she was basically a 'North East Coast' collier, but her design was specially modified prior to construction to suit urgent Admiralty requirements for a vessel to carry the large turrets for the 14-inch guns fitted to the *King George V* class battleships, then under construction on Tyne, Mersey and Clyde, from the Vickers armament works at Barrow. The major change made was to increase the beam of the vessel by some two feet from 44.5 feet to 46.7 feet and, although not evident from the photograph, the hatches were also lengthened to 76 feet. To make this modification, it would appear that numbers 1 and 2, and 3 and 4 holds were combined to make two large compartments. In addition the coamings of one hatch had circular bulges on each side to accommodate the barbettes of a four-gun turret which measured 22.5 feet in diameter. Other modifications shown in the photograph include the provision of masts at the ends

The 1931-built *Dalewood* (top) was not as fortunate during the Second World War as *Chelwood*. On 20th August 1941 she was torpedoed by German surface forces off the Norfolk coast during a ballast voyage from London to the Tyne. She was towed into the Humber, but was so badly damaged aft that she needed a new engine, being returned to service in March 1942. She then soldiered on until 1958, when the first of a long list of Greek and later Italian owners truncated her name to *Dale*. Fourteen years and five further names later, she was broken up during 1972 at La Spezia. [*Roy Fenton collection*]

Goodwood of 1937 (middle) was one of the earliest sinkings in the Second World War, mined on 10th September 1939 one mile south east of Flamborough Head whilst on a voyage from the Tyne to Bayonne with coal. [*David Whiteside collection*]

Hawkwood of 1934 (right) was another collier lost on the east coast during the Second World War. On 26th January 1942 she stranded on Seaton Sands, Tees Bay whilst on a voyage from Blyth to London with coal. [*David Whiteside collection*]

of each hatch to take heavy lift derricks, and a crow's nest fitted on the foremast. The wheelhouse and the bridge cabs port and starboard have been given some form of protection against enemy attack and emergency life rafts provided, but there is no sign of defensive armament. Presumably the structures port and starboard at the bridge front are part of the special cargo handling equipment.

These specific changes apart, it will be seen that the post-depression 'aesthetic' improvements evident in the design of the larger tramp ships, and referred to in 'Record' 50, were also carried through to the colliers, with a raked stem and cruiser stern particular features, along with a more rounded deckhouse and a shorter funnel. *Sea Fisher* was actually built for a new company (Fenwick, Fisher Steam Ship Co. Ltd.), jointly formed by France, Fenwick, and James Fisher of Barrow-on-Furness, the latter regularly operating vessels on charter to the Admiralty to carry gun

mountings and other specialist naval equipment. A year after her completion, the Admiralty received a scare when the vessel was severely damaged when hitting a mine off the north east coast of England and would have sunk had she been loaded. A reserve vessel was immediately ordered and was delivered to the Fenwick, Fisher company as *Sound Fisher* in October 1941. Records show that *Sea Fisher* delivered gun mountings for HMS *Prince of Wales*, *Duke of York* and *Howe* between June 1940 and May 1942. When not required by the Admiralty, both vessels were employed as colliers. After the war, the Fenwick, Fisher company was liquidated and *Sea Fisher* was transferred to James Fisher ownership with *Sound Fisher* joining France, Fenwick as *Portwood*, and a post-war aerial photograph of this ship shows that at some stage she had been converted back to a four hold/four hatch collier, with most of the heavy lift gear removed.

Sea Fisher's sister *Sound Fisher* was completed in October 1941. The Fenwick, Fisher Steam Ship Co. Ltd. appears to have been wound up in 1945, and she was transferred to France, Fenwick. There was little time to give her a company name as in March 1946 she was transferred to Coastwise Colliers Ltd., London, a joint venture with Stephenson Clarke and William Cory to charter colliers to the County of London Electricity Supply Company. The company's nine colliers were given names beginning 'Col' from the initials of the electricity company, *Sound Fisher* becoming *Colnbrook*. On nationalisation of the electricity industry, Coastwise Colliers was wound up, and in 1949 the ship took the France, Fenwick name *Portwood* (above), which she was to keep until sold to Greek

owners in 1962 as *Chrysanthi K*, seen above sailing from Preston. An engine room fire in December 1966 sealed her fate, but there was unseemly delay in demolishing her and

only after she had passed through the hands of at least three breakers did scrapping begin at Santander in 1969. *[Roy Fenton collection; J. and M. Clarkson]*

The 1930s was the period when, with war clouds gathering, the Admiralty began to look at current merchant ship designs in order to produce a portfolio of those which could be developed as 'standards' for relatively easy construction if required, and France, Fenwick were proud that their up-dated *Chelwood* design was selected as the prototype for the 4,100 tons deadweight class collier. A number of these were built during the war, and the series continued into peacetime as owners sought to replace tonnage lost during the conflict. In appearance, these vessels were similar to *Sea Fisher* (excluding its Admiralty extras, of course). However, although the basic parameters remained, a more modern outline was developed for vessels loading around 4,500 tons deadweight which began to appear in the 1950s. In the fullness of time these modifications would include the use of oil fuel and eventually diesel propulsion. The nationalisation of the coal, gas and electricity industries had changed domestic trading patterns and the export market had all but disappeared, forcing owners like France, Fenwick to look elsewhere for business, consequently the last few vessels built to the basic *Chelwood* design included features making them suitable for deep-sea trading.

Separately, just as they had done with the engines aft/raised quarter deck design some thirty years earlier, shipbuilders were overcoming the technical difficulties surrounding the development of larger single-deck vessels and, as a result, the next series of colliers were generally of this type, capable of carrying cargoes ranging from 5,000 tons deadweight to the ultimate 19,000 tons. By this time oil and natural gas, and the ending of the British coal industry and the substitution of its products by imported coal, had brought the centuries old 'North East Coast Coal Trade' to an end, and the last few derivatives of the original *Chelwood* design which remained were disposed of. The name *Chelwood*, however, was carried on by one of these larger vessels, a 7,727 tons deadweight, single deck/machinery aft collier, built by Bartram and Sons at Sunderland, which entered service in 1964.

SOURCES AND ACKNOWLEDGEMENTS

We thank all who gave permission for their photographs to be used, and for help in finding photographs we are particularly grateful to Tony Smith, Jim McFaul and David Whiteside of the World Ship Photo Library; to Ian Farquhar, F.W. Hawks, Peter Newall, William Schell; and to David Hodge and Bob Todd of the National Maritime Museum, and other museums and institutions listed.

Research sources have included the *Registers* of William Schell and Tony Starke, 'Lloyd's Register', 'Lloyd's Confidential Index', 'Lloyd's Shipping Index', 'Lloyd's War Losses', 'Mercantile Navy Lists', 'Marine News', 'Sea Breezes' and 'Shipbuilding and Shipping Record'. Use of the facilities of the World Ship Society, the Guildhall Library, the National Archives and Lloyd's Register of Shipping and the help of Dr Malcolm Cooper are gratefully acknowledged. Particular thanks also to Heather Fenton for editorial and indexing work, and to Marion Clarkson for accountancy services.

Hog Island Three
The Schell/Starke indexes were the basis of the ships' careers, with additional details from 'Lloyd's Register' and British registration documents in class BT110 at the National Archives, Kew. Voyage details are from the Voyage Record Cards, part of the Lloyd's Collection at the Guildhall Library, London. Much background information came from Mark H. Goldberg's 'The Hog Islanders', published by the American Merchant Marine Museum, Kings Point, New York in 1991.

Hopemount Shipping Co. Ltd.
Thanks to David Burrell. Sources include Swan, Hunter and Wigham Richardson's house magazine 'The Shipbuilder'; material in Tyne and Wear Archives, Newcastle-upon-Tyne; various World Ship Society fleet histories; and www.convoyweb.org.uk

Austin's 'Chelwood' Type Colliers
The main sources of information were the official company history of Wm. France, Fenwick and Co. Ltd., published in 1954, and subsequently serialised in 'Sea Breezes', and 'The Steam Collier Fleets' by Captain J.A. MacRae and C.V. Waine. The photographs by Frank and Sons were commissioned by S.P. Austin and Sons Ltd., Sunderland and given to the author. Other photographs are credited separately. References to *Sea Fisher*'s wartime Admiralty voyages were published in the World Ship Society 'Warships Supplement' No. 155 (2007) and supplied by Dr. I.L. Buxton.

The French Bounty Ship Boom 1897-1902
John's drafting of captions to the photographs was at an early stage, and we have had to base these on his notes, information on the backs of the photographs, and - to a large extent –Schell's 'Register of Steel Merchant Sailing Vessels Built 1890 to 1930'.
Sources known to have been used by John for his article include:
Frank G.B. Carr et al 'The Medley of Mast and Sail: A Camera Record' Toredo Books, Brighton, 1976 (volume I), 1981 (volume II)
Robert Gardiner (editor) 'Sail's Last Century: The Merchant Sailing Ship 1830-1930' Conway, London, 1993.
Alex A. Hurst 'Square Riggers – The Final Epoch 1921-1958' Toredo Books, Brighton, 1974
Louis Lacroix 'Les Dernier Grands Voiliers' Amîot-Dumont, Paris, 1950.
Louis Lacroix 'L'Age d'Or de la Voile' Second edition, Jean-Pierre Gyss, Strasbourg, 1999.
Brigitte et Yvonne Le Coat 'Cap-Horniers Français' (Two volumes) La Chasse-Marée/ Éditions Ouset- France, Rennes/ Douarnenez, 2002-3
Basil Lubbock 'The Nitrate Clippers' Brown, Son and Ferguson, Glasgow, 1932
Jean Randier 'Men and Ships around Cape Horn 1616-1939' Arthur Barker, London, 1968.
Jean Randier 'Grands Voiliers Français 1880-1930' Éditions de Quatre Seigneurs, Grenoble, 1974
Graham West 'Madeleine and the bounty' Windjammer, 2003, 4, 13-17.
Ulrich Schaefer 'Die deutschen Grosssegler: Eine Strukturanalyse fur die jahre 1900 und 1914', Der Albatros, Heft 2, 2006, 63-70.
Alan Villiers and Henri Picard 'The Bounty Ships of France', Patrick Stephens, London, 1972.
John also refered to various editions of the journals Log Chips and the Annual Dog Watch.

HOPEMOUNT SHIPPING CO. LTD. Part 1

Ian Rae

This article refers mainly to ships of this Tyneside-based tramp fleet which was largely owned by the shipbuilder Swan, Hunter and Wigham Richardson Ltd. All Hopemount's ships were built on the Tyne at Swan, Hunter's Wallsend and Neptune yards, on the Wear at their Southwick yard, or by their subsidiary Barclay, Curle and Co. Ltd. on the Clyde. Many were speculative ventures, built in the hope that owners would seize the chance of not having to wait for their own orders to be fulfilled, and have a ready-made ship for their trades. It is claimed that Swan, Hunter - wanting to keep costs down on ships building for this owner - used mostly apprentice labour in their construction.

Over sixty years Hopemount would own twenty cargo ships and two tankers. The company would have their share of ups and downs and, like all others, be subjected to the vagaries of freight rate fluctuations, while their ships tramped for cargoes world wide. As the ships had individual characteristics, the narrative will take each in turn and describe its career up to its sale by Hopemount or associated companies, the accompanying fleet list giving further details of its life and fate.

Origins

At the start of the twentieth century Swan, Hunter and Wigham Richardson Ltd. were steered to world wide fame by their Chairman George Burton Hunter. He was the moving force in setting up Hopemount Shipping Co. Ltd., and over the next six decades directors of this company came from the builders' boardroom, from the shipping company's managing agents, or were shipping personalities from Tyneside.

It was a characteristic of the industry in the late nineteenth century that shipbuilders constructed ships 'on spec' to keep their yards employed, as contemporary vessels were simple cargo ships with few refinements and which could be readily modified if required when an owner came along. In addition, ship owners would trade in their older ships to builders in part payment for new tonnage, and the builder would sell on the older ships to third parties, or operate them themselves. Swan, Hunter continued with this practice well into the twentieth century.

George Hunter had become a partner in C.S. Swan and Hunter Company in 1895 and took on the role of Chairman. It is assumed that this is how he became owner of the passenger-cargo ship *Belgian King* (3,393/1881). As *Connemara* she had been owned by Ralph M. Hudson of John Street, Sunderland until July 1893 when she passed to Hunter. Around this time Hudson ordered two ships from the builder: the 6,850-grt *Westmeath* launched on 27th July 1895 and the 4,284-grt *Leitrim* launched on 14th February 1896. Presumably the builders accepted *Connemara* in part payment for the two new ships, as Swan, Hunter went on to replace her two-cylinder compound engine with a new triple-expansion set made by the Wallsend Slipway Co. Ltd. She was renamed *Belgian King* continuing under Hunter's personal ownership and management by Elder, Dempster until 1901 when she was sold. Hunter offered her buyers a mortgage, and when they defaulted on payment he took her back, in partnership with C.S. Swan. She was later managed

in Constantinople until she foundered in September 1914 near Cape Kureli. Hunter's 1893 acquisition of the ship may have been the catalyst that encouraged the venture into ship owning by the newly integrated company of Swan, Hunter and Wigham Richardson Ltd. of which Hunter had become Chairman in 1903. Latterly managed by Stamp, Mann and Co., *Belgian King* is included as an appendix to the fleet list.

On 11th February 1904 the builder's board authorised a 5,400 deadweight ship to be built 'on spec', which would be allocated the yard number 713. On 16th June 1904 the contract for the ship was transferred to George M. Stamp and Arthur Mann, two local shipping men who would manage the new Hopemount company under the title Stamp, Mann and Co. She was expected to be launched on the same day, but this was delayed until 21st June because of high winds. Whilst fitting out, the steamer was used to test a floating dock for Port Said, which the Wallsend yard had just completed. *Hopemount* cost £35,712, making Swan, Hunter a profit of £628. The Hopemount Shipping Co. Ltd. was established on the day of the launch, with the vast majority of its £12,000 capital owned by the builders. Although the capital was later greatly increased, to over £400,000 by 1960, Swan, Hunter and Wigham Richardson Ltd. remained the principal shareholder, and also provided mortgages for the majority of the Hopemount ships

Hopemount (1) was transferred to the new company on 11th July, with Stamp, Mann and Co., appointed as managers. By the thirteenth A.G.M. of the Hopemount Shipping Co. Ltd., the status of George Stamp and Arthur Mann had changed in that they were appointed directors. As a typical tramp, *Hopemount* followed a familiar trading pattern, taking coal from the Northumberland, Durham and South Wales coalfields to Mediterranean ports, including Genoa, Leghorn, Alexandria and Port Said. She would then proceed in ballast to Black Sea ports such as Odessa, Azov and Novorossisk to bring grain back to the UK and continental ports. Her forty sixth voyage was to be her last. Sailing from Cardiff for Alexandria and Karachi with coal, on 13th June 1915 *Hopemount* (1) was captured and sunk in the Bristol Channel by *U 35*. This U-boat was one of the most successful in the Kriegsmarine sinking a total of 224 ships of 539,741 tons. At the twelfth AGM of Hopemount Shipping it was decided that, due to the high costs of second-hand tonnage following the First World War, *Hopemount* (1) would not be replaced immediately.

Colliers

In June 1917 the Hopemount Company took a half share in the 590-deadweight collier *Northwick*, which had been completed by Swan, Hunter and Wigham Richardson Ltd. at Southwick, a yard on the River Wear re-opened in 1912. On completion *Northwick* was requisitioned by the Shipping Controller, and up to December 1918 the owners made £8,492 profit on her, and then sold her as the post-war second-hand market boomed.

In 1918 Hopemount's share capital was raised to £53,000 to pay for two 3,500 deadweight colliers being built in the Sunderland yard, *Hopelyn* and *Hopecrest*, both of

A trial's view of *Hopemount* (1) of 1904, the company's first ship. Note the long bridge deck and the exceptionally narrow bridge structure. *[Author's collection]*

which were to come to dramatic ends. Resuming her east coast work following Admiralty requisition, *Hopelyn* was wrecked on Scorby Sands on 19th October 1922 after her steering gear failed during a north easterly gale. Only valiant efforts by the Gorleston and Lowestoft lifeboats prevented a total disaster, saving 24 members of the crew. The lifeboat coxswains and crews received two gold and 25 other medals for the rescue.

Hopecrest was sold to Cory Colliers Ltd. after the war and renamed *Corcrest*. During the Second World War she had an adventurous time, as part of the convoy OS 50/ KMS17 taking stores to Algiers in June 1943 and later transporting petrol cans around the Mediterranean.

In February 1948 she was extensively damaged in collision with Elder, Dempster's *Freetown* (5,853/1928) in the Thames. Worse was to follow on 21st June 1949 when, on passage from Rochester to the Wear in ballast, she struck the wreck of the *Fort Massac* (7,157/1943). This Canadian steamer had sunk in relatively shallow water following a collision on 1st February 1946 with the Hebburn-built motor coaster *Thornaby* (1,174/1935). *Corcrest* struck the submerged wreck and straddled it, sticking fast with two of her holds ruptured. Despite attempts to pull her off by Thames tugs, she remained there until the two wrecks were blown up by Trinity House some years later.

In 1919 the demand for ships continued to grow and freight rates remained high; raw materials were needed for reconstruction, ships lost or damaged during the war needed replacing. But the boom was short lived as freight rates collapsed in the summer of 1920, and continued in a downward spiral for five years, by which time large numbers of ships were laid up. Freight rate fluctuations were always the main topic in reports of Hopemount annual general meetings. One of the few occasions on which the reports sounded optimistic was during the miners' dispute which continued long after the UK's short-lived general strike and 'which brought a brisk demand for coal from the U.S.A'.

The *Hopecrest* (1), second of two colliers completed in 1918, became Cory's *Corcrest* just over a year later. *Corcrest* is seen in wartime. Although surviving a Luftwaffe attack in August 1941, she did not long survive the peace, sinking after hitting a wreck in June 1949. *[National Maritime Museum]*

The steamer *Hopeland* of 1923 was completed at a difficult time for tramp shipping, and after indifferent trading results was sold in 1928. Note the straight hances where her bulwarks change height. *[Nautical Photo Agency/Roy Fenton collection]*

In October 1921 the coalition government led by Lloyd George passed the Trade Facility Act 1922 aimed at reflating the economy and reducing unemployment by stimulating the engineering and shipbuilding industries. The act allowed the Treasury to guarantee loans for capital undertakings and for the purchase of British manufactured goods. Although there was a change in Government in 1922, the scheme continued until 1927, whilst in Northern Ireland a local scheme lasted until 1953.

Against this economic and political background Hopemount Shipping ordered a replacement for the *Hopelyn* from Swan, Hunter's Clydeside subsidiary, Barclay, Curle. Launched in October 1923, *Hopeland* was not a commercial success, with many of her return voyages being completed in ballast. She was sold in 1928.

Motor ship misery

During the 1920s shipbuilders were adopting innovative engineering solutions to reduce operating costs and increase efficiency, but by no means all were successful.

In 1913 amongst other acquisitions Swan, Hunter had bought the Clydeside shipbuilder Barclay, Curle and Co. Ltd., who had acquired the North British Diesel Engine Works from Dr. Rudolf Diesel in 1909. After a mixed record in developing diesel engines, the works' Chief Designer, J.C.M. MacLagan, designed a two-stroke, double-acting engine, which was fitted into several Barclay, Curle-built ships (see 'Record' 16 for a

detailed description of this machinery). The contemporary shipping press limited itself to fulsome praise of new designs, rarely hinting at the problems they often had in service. In the event, all the MacLagan-engined ships turned out to be spectacular and costly failures. None of their operators was satisfied with their performance, complaining of numerous engine breakdowns, and it was finally agreed that all three ships would be re-engined at the builder's expense.

The first of these was *Swanley*, the first British-built ship powered by a double-acting diesel engine. She was built at a cost of £110,000 for the Swanley Shipping Co. Ltd., a joint venture of Harris and Dixon Ltd. and the Swan, Hunter and Wigham Richardson group of companies, running trials during June 1924. The maiden voyage of

A pioneering motor ship, *Swanley* of 1924 proved a mechanical disaster and was re-engined in 1927. *[J. and M. Clarkson collection]*

Swanley began on 5th July 1924 at Cardiff where she loaded coal, and was to last six months during which she covered 18,000 miles on her route via Port Said to Colombo, arriving on 5th August 1924, averaging 9.7 knots on 6.9 tons of fuel per day. However, recurring engineering problems became a major issue and following an inspection at Kiel where her bearings were found to be seriously scored, she was returned to her builders. In 1927 her original engines were replaced with a three-cylinder Doxford-type diesel licence-built by Barclay, Curle and Co. Ltd. The Swan, Hunter shareholding in the Swanley Shipping Co. Ltd. was increased to 75% and eventually to full control in 1932, when she was transferred to Hopemount Shipping Co. Ltd. and renamed *Hoperange*. She was sold to Norwegian owners in 1937, operating successfully until torpedoed in September 1940.

Another of the MacLagan failures was launched un-named from the Clydeside yard at the end of March 1925, and whilst fitting out acquired the name *Frederick Gilbert*. Having run successful trials, she was taken on a three-year charter by Sir John Ellerman as *City of Stockholm*, with an option to buy. However, on 1st March 1927 Ellermans told the builders that they intended to cancel the charter, returning the ship on account of her unsatisfactory machinery. Later that month Hopemount Shipping purchased her and brought her to the Tyne, where a new steam engine was fitted at Swan's Neptune Engine Works. Subsequently the ship was sold to Venatus Shipping Co. Ltd. and re-named *Prunus*, but due to the continuing depression this company defaulted on mortgage payments and the steamer was repossessed by Hopemount Shipping who renamed her *Hopetor*, finally selling her to Barry Shipping Co. Ltd. in 1936.

Motor ship success

In their own right Swan, Hunter held a licence to build Swedish Polar oil engines and produced an improved version at their Neptune works. This went into another speculative build at Wallsend. Launched un-named in 1925, she later became *Neptunian*, echoing the name of her six-cylinder Neptune diesel engine which gave her a trial speed of 11.49 knots.

On completion *Neptunian* was chartered to a Norwegian owner, who had an option to buy her, and used on a service from Scandinavia to the River Plate. But after two years the Norwegian did not take up the option to purchase the ship, which was returned to the builders. On 22nd August 1928, Hopemount Shipping received the £60,000 which had been borrowed from the Treasury under the Trades Facilities Act, with the ship mortgaged to the Treasury. Unusually, W.A. Souter and Co. Ltd. were appointed in place of Stott as managers of *Neptunian*. She was torpedoed on 6th September 1940 north west of Rockall, still with her original diesel engine.

Hopemount Shipping's single-minded concentration on the traditional dry cargo trade ended following a Swan, Hunter Board meeting in February 1928, when a ten-year charter from Anglo-Saxon Petroleum Co. Ltd.

was agreed for a 11,000 deadweight diesel tanker. In January 1929 Hopemount Shipping entered into a tripartite agreement with Swan, Hunter and Anglo-Saxon for the ship which became *Hopemount* (2). Unlike the other early motor ships, she traded without incident, and in the early years of the Second World War carried creosote from the West Indies, and later fuel oil for the U.S. warships operating in the Eastern Atlantic. On frequent occasions she would act as the escort oiler for the convoys.

On 27th March 1942 *Hopemount* (2) sailed from Oban to join the convoy PQ 14 to Murmansk, consisting of 25 merchant ships and 40 escorts. After sailing from Reykjavik on 8th April the convoy endured 30 hours of thick fog and 12 hours of heavy pack ice, forcing the return to Iceland of the majority of the ships, *Hopemount* being one of only eight to continue. Persistent attacks were made by aircraft, submarines and destroyers, although these succeeded in sinking only one ship, that of the convoy commodore, *Empire Howard* (6,985/1941). Battered and weary, *Hopemount* and the other six ships arrived at Murmansk on 19th April.

The Ministry of War Transport then loaned *Hopemount* to Russia who sent her along the Siberian coast as far as Tikse Bay to fuel a small flotilla of Russian destroyers coming round from Vladivostok. She was used as a replenishment ship, mainly based at Iokanka, for most of 1942, propeller and bow damage restricting her speed to six knots. Rear Admiral Douglas Fisher, who was in charge of the operations in the area, has described the rigid and paranoid regulations that the Russians thought up to make it almost impossible for personnel to leave the country. *Hopemount* arrived back at Loch Ewe on 11th January 1943. She was then refitted on the Tyne, after which she made 14 trips across the Atlantic as an escort oiler, also supplying fuel to Londonderry and Scapa Flow. At the end of the war she was sold to Anglo-Saxon Petroleum Co. Ltd. and renamed *Kelletia*, the deal giving Hopemount a profit of £80,534.

Steam and diesel

In 1927 the management of Hopemount Shipping passed to Arthur Stott and Co. Ltd., when George Stamp and Arthur Mann retired from the business. Established in 1921, Arthur Stott and Co. Ltd. also managed vessels for other shipping

Hopemount (2) was the first oil tanker to join the fleet. When sold to Shell in 1945 to fill in for war losses until the new 'H' class came into service, she made a profit of £80,534 for Hopemount. *[J. and M. Clarkson collection]*

companies, including two ships for the International South American Steam Ship Co. Ltd. and one for the Monkseaton Steamship Co. Ltd. The latter had the Arch-deck steamer *Murie S* (1,701/1923), which had been repossessed by Swan, Hunter as builders and mortgagees. The Mann involvement continued, as a Leslie Mann became managing director and in registration documents is listed as the manager, the person responsible for the ships. Reorganisation of the management company would see it become Stott, Mann and Fleming Ltd. in 1938, and Stott, Mann Co. Ltd. in April 1954. It held a minority shareholding in Hopemount Shipping Co. Ltd.

In early 1929 Hopemount Shipping ordered two 6,750-deadweight dry cargo ships from the Southwick yard, each at a contract price of £64,500 for the hull and £17,300 for the machinery. *Hopecrag* was the first to enter service and, despite the desperate trading conditions, she obtained a two-year charter in Far Eastern waters. This was followed by an eventful voyage to Russia. Leaving Murmansk on 21st July 1936, with 800 tons of bunkers she sailed in thick fog in a five-ship convoy through the Kara Sea led by the icebreaker *Lenin*. The destination was the Yenisei River in Siberia, where they arrived at Igarka on 31st, the signal station's hoist welcoming the first convoy of the year. Here they were subjected to Stalin's propaganda, with the jetty decorated with red bunting and flags, and placards with Stalin's image inviting the workers of the world to unite. It took eleven days to load a cargo of timber, which had been brought down the 2,500-mile river on barges.

For the westward voyage there were no icebreakers available, so passage was slow and at times the ship had to drift with the ice. She discharged at the end of August in Hull. In 1938 *Hopecrag* was sold to Norwegians, taking the name *Wyvern*.

The second ship of the pair, *Hopedene*, launched by the wife of the Managing Director of Hopemount Shipping Co. Ltd., had a fairly routine career. In 1938 she too was sold, going for £46,755 to Stag Line of North Shields, who renamed her *Photinia*.

The difficult times being experienced by the shipping industry were exacerbated by the Wall Street Crash of November 1929. This meant Hopemount Shipping did not venture into the depressed shipbuilding arena again until July 1934 when they ordered a 9,500-deadweight cargo ship from Barclay, Curle. The Glasgow yard's engine works had built a Doxford engine as a speculative venture to keep the labour force employed, and this was fitted to the new *Hopecrest*.

When war was declared in September 1939 *Hopecrest* was loading wool at Port Stanley for the UK. This was followed by eleven voyages across the Atlantic, with cargoes of timber and grain from Vancouver and sugar from Cuba. In 1942 she carried a cargo comprising millstones, aircraft, ammunition and other military stores to Casablanca as part of the build up for Operation Torch. Later that year she brought to the UK an unusual cargo of Jerry Cans and scrap steel from Alexandria and Haifa. *Hopecrest* was sold to German owners in 1951.

To be concluded.

Despite being launched at an unpropitious time, the steamer *Hopecrag* of 1929 traded reasonably successfully for Hopemount until sold in 1938. *[Roy Fenton collection]*

Hopemount Shipping Co. Ltd.
(Stamp, Mann and Co., managers)
Newcastle-upon-Tyne

Fleet list
Ships are listed in the order in which they entered the Hopemount fleet.

1. **HOPEMOUNT** (1) 1904-1915
O.N. 118641 3,300g 2,105n 5,651d.
331.3 x 49.0 x 22.6 feet.
T. 3-cyl by North Eastern Marine Engineering Co. Ltd., Wallsend-on-Tyne (23, 38, 64 x 45 inches), 350 NHP, 1,700 IHP, 10.5 knots.
4.3.1904: Laid down.
21.6.1904: Launched by Swan, Hunter and Wigham Richardson Ltd., Wallsend-on-Tyne (Yard No. 713).
31.7.1904: Completed.
15.9.1904: Registered in the ownership of Hopemount Shipping Co. Ltd. (Stamp, Mann and Co., managers), Newcastle-upon-Tyne as HOPEMOUNT.
13.6.1915: Captured and sunk by gunfire from the German submarine U 35 seventy miles west by south of Lundy whilst on a voyage from Cardiff to Alexandria and Karachi with a cargo of coal. Her master was badly wounded during the attack.
2.7.1915: Register closed.

2. **NORTHWICK** 1917-1919
O.N. 137262 472g 236n 590d.
158.2 x 26.0 x 11.75 (depth), 10.9 (draft) feet.
T. 3-cyl. by William Beardmore and Co. Ltd., Glasgow.
22.8.1916: Laid down.
7.5.1917: Launched by Swan, Hunter and Wigham Richardson Ltd., Southwick, Sunderland (Yard No. 1033).
5.6.1917: Ran trials and subsequently completed for Hopemount Shipping Co. Ltd., Newcastle-upon-Tyne (32/64) and Pile and Co. Ltd., London (32/64) (Stamp, Mann and Co. Ltd., Newcastle-upon-Tyne, managers) as NORTHWICK.
1919: Sold to Coombes, Marshall and Co. Ltd., Middlesbrough and renamed ESKBURN.
1926: Transferred to Coombes (Middlesbrough) Ltd.
1928: Sold to William G. James (William G. James and Sons, managers), Cardigan.
1935: Transferred to British Isles Coasters Ltd. , Cardigan.
1941: Sold to the Efford Shipping Co. Ltd., London.
1946: Renamed SPRINGBURN.
1947: Sold to F. Bowles and Sons Ltd. (J. Bowles, manager), Cardiff.
1948: Converted to a sand pump dredger, renamed SUNFOLD and manager became David M. Bowles.
10.5.1961: Arrived at Swansea for breaking up by the Prince of Wales Dry Dock Co. Ltd.

Hopemount (1) was an early U-boat victim. *[Bristol Series/J. and M. Clarkson collection]*

After a long career as a coaster, the former *Northwick* was bought by a Cardiff company in 1947 and converted into the sand pump dredger *Sunfold*, prolonging her life until 1961. *[Both: World Ship Society Ltd.]*

3. **HOPELYN** 1918-1922
O.N. 140706 2,348g 1,301n 3,500d.
284.5 x 41.5 x 19.1 feet.
T. 3-cyl. (22, 35, 58 x 39 inches) by
the Neptune Engine Works of Swan,
Hunter and Wigham Richardson Ltd.,
Low Walker; 249 NHP, 1,500 IHP, 11
knots.
29.1.1917: Laid down by Swan, Hunter
and Wigham Richardson Ltd., Southwick,
Sunderland (Yard No. 1041).
20.12.1917: Launched.
18.2.1918: Registered in the ownership
of Hopemount Shipping Co. Ltd.
(Stamp, Mann and Co., managers),
Newcastle-upon-Tyne as HOPELYN.
19.2.1918: Ran trials.
Requisitioned on delivery by the
Shipping Controller until 14.5.1918.
19.10.1922: Wrecked on Scorby Sands
whilst on a voyage from the Tyne to
the Thames with a cargo of 3,400 tons
of coal.
10.11.1922: Register closed.

4. **HOPECREST** (1) 1918-1919
O.N.140715 2,373g 1,337n 3,525d.
285.9 x 41.3 x 21.3 (depth), 19.2 (draft)
feet.
T.3-cyl. (22, 35, 58 x 39 inches) by
the Neptune Engine Works of Swan,
Hunter and Wigham Richardson Ltd.,
Low Walker; 288 NHP, 1,650 IHP, 11.5
knots.
9.5.1917: Laid down by Swan,
Hunter and Wigham Richardson Ltd.,

Hopelyn was the first of two colliers completed in 1918. *[National Maritime Museum P10868]*

Southwick, Sunderland (Yard No. 1051).
27.3.1918: Launched.
13.5.1918: Registered in the ownership of the
Hopemount Shipping Co. Ltd. (Stamp, Mann
and Co. Ltd., managers), Newcastle-upon-Tyne
as HOPECREST.
15.5.1918: Ran trials and completed.
27.5.1919: Acquired by Cory Colliers Ltd.,
London.
25.6.1919: Renamed CORCREST.
1932: Managers became William Cory and Son
Ltd.

8.1941: Damaged in an air attack whilst on a
voyage from Blyth to the Thames.
30.3.1946: Transferred to William Cory and
Son Ltd., London.
21.6.1949: Struck the wreck of the steamer
FORT MASSAC (7,157/1943) 2.5 miles
north west by west of the Sunk Light Vessel,
abandoned and subsequently sank. She was on
a ballast voyage from Rochester to Sunderland.
23.6.1949: Abandoned as a total loss.
1.7.1949: Register closed.

Corcrest, formerly *Hopecrest* (1) in Cory ownership before the Second World War. *[Ships in Focus]*

5. HOPELAND 1923-1928

O.N. 148043 4,281g 2,662n 7,830d.
370.6 x 53.0 x 25.2 feet.
T. 3-cyl. (24, 40, 65 x 45 inches) by
Barclay, Curle and Co. Ltd., Glasgow;
276 NHP, 1,800 IHP, 10.5 knots.
12.10.1923: Launched by Barclay,
Curle and Co. Ltd., Glasgow (Yard No.
597).
7.11.1923: Registered in the
ownership of Hopemount Shipping
Co. Ltd. (Stamp, Mann and Co. Ltd.,
managers), Newcastle-upon-Tyne as
HOPELAND.
26.12.1928: Sold to Prentice, Service
and Henderson, Glasgow.
26.3.1929: Renamed CROWN OF
GALICIA.
2.4.1935: Sold to Alexander Shipping
Co. Ltd. (Capper, Alexander and Co.,
managers), London.
9.4.1935: Renamed SHAFTESBURY.
12.7.1942: Torpedoed and sunk by
the German submarine U 116 off the
Azores in position 31.42 north, 25.30
west whilst on a voyage from Newport
to Buenos Aires with a cargo of coal
after convoy OS 33 had dispersed.
26.10.1942: Register closed.

Hopeland seen after sale in 1929 and renaming *Crown of Galicia* (above). In 1935 she was sold again and renamed *Shaftesbury* (below) and is seen in Australian waters. *[J. and M. Clarkson; Warwick Foote/Roy Fenton collection]*

6. CITY OF STOCKHOLM/HOPETOR
1927, 1932-1937

O.N. 147326 5,017g 3,124n 9,433d.
418.5 x 55.4 x 26.3 feet.
2SCDA 3-cyl. (24.5 x 44 inches) MacLagan-
type diesel engine by North British Diesel
Engine Works (1922) Ltd., Glasgow; 1,890
BHP, 2,250 IHP, 10½ knots.
1927: T. 3-cyl. (25.5, 42 and 70 x 48 inches)
by the Neptune Engine Works of Swan,
Hunter and Wigham Richardson Ltd., Low
Walker; 505 NHP, 3,100 IHP; 11.75 knots.

31.3.1925: Launched by Barclay, Curle and
Co. Ltd., Scotstoun, Glasgow (Yard No. 608).
Whilst fitting out named FREDERICK
GILBERT.
27.8.1925: Registered in the ownership
of Hall Line Ltd., Liverpool (Ellerman
Lines Ltd., London, managers) as CITY
OF STOCKHOLM. This was a bareboat
charter, intended to last for three years.
29.8.1925: Ran trials and completed.
30.3.1927: Acquired by Hopemount
Shipping Co. Ltd. (Stamp, Mann and Co.

Ltd., managers), Newcastle-upon-Tyne
1927: Re-engined by the Neptune Engine
Works at the builders' expense.
31.9.1927: Sold to Venatus Shipping Co.
Ltd. (Howard Tenens Ltd., managers),
London for £85,000.
3.10.1927: Renamed PRUNUS.
1.12.1932: Re-acquired by Hopemount
Shipping Co. Ltd. (A. Stott and Co. Ltd.,
managers), Newcastle-on-Tyne when owners
defaulted on mortgage payments.
6.12.1932: Renamed HOPETOR.

16.7.1937: Sold to Barry Shipping Co. Ltd.
(B. and S. Steam Shipping Co. Ltd.), Cardiff
for about £49,000.
22.7.1937: Renamed ST. MERRIEL.
17.4.1939: Owners restyled South American
Saint Line Ltd.
2.1.1943: Bombed and sunk by German
aircraft at Bone, while discharging.
12.1.1943: Register closed.
12.12.1948: Refloated and beached.
4.8.1950: Afterpart foundered off Cape Noli
whilst in tow for breakers at Savona.

7. NEPTUNIAN 1927-1940
O.N. 149426 5,155g 3,208n 9,010d.
400.3 x 55.4 x 27.2 feet.
2SCSA 6-cyl. (24 x 50 inches) oil engine by
the Neptune Engine Works of Swan, Hunter
and Wigham Richardson Ltd., Low Walker;
598 BHP, 2,400 BHP, 11 knots.
7.6.1924: Laid down by Swan, Hunter
and Wigham Richardson Ltd., Wallsend
Shipyard (Yard No. 1255).
23.1.1925: Launched un-named.
7.7.1925: Ran trials as NEPTUNIAN, 11.49
knots.
On completion bareboat chartered to
A/S Valhal (T.H. Skogland & Son A/S),
Haugesund, Norway.
8.4.1927: Registered in the ownership of
Hopemount Shipping Co. Ltd. (Stamp,
Mann and Co. Ltd., managers), Newcastle-
upon-Tyne.
19.8.1927: Managers became W.A. Souter
and Co. Ltd., Newcastle-upon-Tyne.
14.3.1936: Transferred to Swan, Hunter and
Wigham Richardson Ltd., Wallsend-on-Tyne
(W.A. Souter and Co. Ltd., Newcastle-upon-
Tyne, managers).
6-7.9.1940: Torpedoed and sunk by the
German submarine U 47 when north west
of Rockall in position 58.27 north, 17.17
west, whilst on a voyage from Santiago via
Sydney, Cape Breton to Liverpool with a
cargo of sugar in convoy SC 2. She sank
in seven minutes with the loss of her entire
complement.
4.2.1941: Register closed.

8. HOPEMOUNT (2) 1929-1945 Tanker
O.N. 149490 7,434g 4,529n 11,210d.
450.8 x 61.1 x 33.3 feet.
2SCSA 6-cyl. (31 x 43 inches) oil engine by
the Wallsend Slipway and Engineering Co.
Ltd., Wallsend-on-Tyne; 11½ knots.
1947: 4SCSA 8-cyl. (650 x 1,400 mm)
Werkspoor-type oil engine by Hawthorn
Leslie and Co. Ltd., Hebburn-on-Tyne.
28.11.1928: Launched by Swan, Hunter
and Wigham Richardson Ltd., Wallsend
Shipyard, Wallsend-on-Tyne (Yard No.
1357) for Hopemount Shipping Co. Ltd. (A.
Stott and Co. Ltd., managers), Newcastle-
upon-Tyne as HOPEMOUNT.
14.2.1929: Ran trials, 11.83 knots.
1944: Sold to Anglo Saxon Petroleum Co.
Ltd., London.
1945: Rename KELLETIA.
1947: Re-engined.
5.1955: Sold for breaking up in Hong Kong

Hopetor was another unsuccessful motor ship and had to be rebuilt as a steamer
at Swan, Hunter's expense. The photograph was taken in Vancouver, judging by
the timber scow alongside. She ran as *Hopetor* from 1932 to 1937. *[Roy Fenton
collection]*

The shelter-deck motor ship *Neptunian* was managed by W.A. Souter and Co. Ltd.,
but is not wearing their funnel colours in this photograph, believed to have been
taken in an Irish port *[J. and M. Clarkson]*

The tanker *Hopemount* (2) was reprieved whilst at the shipbreakers in 1955, and
was rebuilt as the ore carrier *Coral River*. In this guise she is seen, above and
opposite top, at Sept Iles, Canada. The conversion gave her almost ten years of
further life. *[Both: J. and M. Clarkson collection]*

but bought by the River Line Ltd., Bermuda (Mollers' Ltd., Hong Kong, managers), converted to an ore carrier and renamed CORAL RIVER with a charter to BISCO.
7.1964: Laid up at Hong Kong.
5.9.1964: Driven aground during Typhoon 'Ruby'.
18.10.1964: Refloated
2.1965: Delivered to shipbreakers in Hong Kong.

9. HOPECRAG 1929-1938

O.N. 161539 4,007g 2,457n 6,750d.
364.5x 50.7x24.4 feet.
T. 3-cyl. (24, 39, 65 x 45 inches) by North Eastern Marine Engineering Co. Ltd., Sunderland; 2,170 IHP.
5.9.1929: Launched by Swan, Hunter and Wigham Richardson Ltd., Southwick, Sunderland (Yard No. 1401) for Hopemount Shipping Co. Ltd. (A. Stott and Co. Ltd., managers), Newcastle-upon-Tyne as HOPECRAG.
4.10.1929: Ran trials, 11.99 knots.
1938: Sold to Borges Rederi A/S (Hans Borge, manager), Tønsberg, Norway and renamed WYVERN.
1953: Sold to Zeta Shipping Co. Ltd. (Mollers' Ltd., managers), Hong Kong for £55,000 and renamed ZETA TRADER.
21.10.1958: Aground 35 miles south of Singapore. Refloated eight days later.
17.1.1959: Laid up in Hong Kong.
3.1959: Sold to Hong Kong Rolling Mills Ltd., Hong Kong for demolition.

10. HOPEDENE 1929-1938

O.N. 161545 4,010g 2,457n 6,750d.
364.5 x 50.7 x 26.8 feet.
T. 3-cyl. (24, 39, 65 x 45 inches) by North Eastern Marine Engineering Co. Ltd., Sunderland; 338 NHP, 2,200 IHP, 10¾ knots.
1.11.1929: Launched by Swan, Hunter and Wigham Richardson Ltd., Southwick, Sunderland (Yard No. 1403). The launching ceremony was performed by Mrs Leslie Mann, the wife of the managing director of Hopemount Shipping Co. Ltd.
18.11.1929: Delivered for £66,193.
23.11.1929: Registered in the ownership of Hopemount Shipping Co. Ltd. (A. Stott and Co. Ltd., managers), Newcastle-upon-Tyne as HOPEDENE.
4.12.1929: Ran trials.
3.10.1938: Sold to Stag Line Ltd. (J. Robinson and Sons, managers), North Shields for £46,755.
8.10.1938: Renamed PHOTINIA.
1948: Converted to oil burning.
22.12.1950: Register closed on sale to Rederi A/B Asta (Arthur Andersson, manager), Mariehamn, Finland for £110,000 and renamed ATLAS.
1956: Manager became Lennart Karlsson.
1968: Sold to Compania de Navigation Pinares S.A., Panama (Nello Patella, Venice, Italy) for £51,000 and registered at Mogadisciu, Somali Republic.
1973: Sold to Brodospas, Yugoslavia.
22.1.1974: Arrived at Split for breaking up.

Hopecrag. [Ships in Focus]

Hopedene ghosts past the camera whilst running trials in December 1929. Her house flag and name pennant hang limply, the latter probably never to be flown again. One wonders what happens to such pennants. *[Author's collection]*

Hopecrag was sold to Stag Line in 1938 and renamed *Photinia* (top).

During the Second World War *Photinia* ran in North Atlantic convoys until 1942, when she began to make regular voyages from Trinidad to Key West, Guantanamo Bay and Mobile and did not return to UK waters until February 1945.

In the summer of 1947, *Photinia* was towed into Calcutta with a damaged propeller shaft. A new 17-foot, five-ton shaft was completed by North Eastern Marine Engineering Co. Ltd. on 4th July and air freighted to Calcutta in a converted Handley-Page Halifax bomber which arrived on 8th July. One week later *Photinia* was back at sea.

Sold in 1950 to a Finnish Company for £110,000, *Photinia* was renamed *Atlas*, retaining a stag on her enlarged replacement funnel for new owners (middle, in the Surrey Commercial Docks, and bottom, in the English Channel).

Retaining the name *Atlas*, she was sold again to a Greek Company in 1968, who put her under the Somali flag.

Still with her original North Eastern Marine Engineering Co. Ltd. triple-expansion engine, *Atlas* was broken up in Split during January 1971. [All: Roy Fenton collection]

11. **HOPERANGE** (1) 1932-1937
O.N. 147681 4,950g 3,058n 9,330d.
418.5 x 55.4 x 26.3 feet.
2SCDA 3-cyl. (24.5 x 44 inches)
MacLagan-type oil engine by North
British Diesel Engine Works (1922)
Ltd., Whiteinch, Glasgow; 2,000 BHP,
10 knots.
1927: 2SCSA, 3-cyl. (580 x 2,320mm)
Doxford 58L3-type opposed-piston oil
engine by Barclay, Curle and Co. Ltd.,
Whiteinch, Glasgow; 2,250 BHP.
22.3.1924: Launched by Barclay, Curle
and Co. Ltd., Whiteinch, Glasgow
(Yard No. 596).
30.6.1924: Ran trials and completed
for Swanley Shipping Co. Ltd. (Harris
and Dixon Ltd., managers), London as
SWANLEY.
17.11.1932: Acquired by the
Hopemount Shipping Co. Ltd. (A. Stott
and Co. Ltd., managers), Newcastle-
upon-Tyne.
6.12.1932: Renamed HOPERANGE.
19.3.1937: Register closed on sale to
D/S A/S Vard (Jacobsen and Salvesen,
managers), Oslo, Norway and later
renamed HIRD.
28.5.1940: Assisted in the evacuation of
almost 4,000 troops and civilians from
Dunkirk.
29.5.1940: Picked up the crew of the
sinking destroyer H.M.S. WAKEFUL
and took them to Cherbourg.
15.9.1940: Torpedoed by the German
submarine U 65 in position 58.00
north, 12.20 west, when a straggler
from convoy HX 72, on a voyage from
Panama City, Mobile and Bermuda to
Manchester, with 8,101 tons of general
cargo and 197 tons black carbon. The
master and crew were picked up by
the Icelandic trawler THOROLFUR
(403/1920) and landed at Fleetwood.

The *Swanley* was renamed *Hopemount* after re-engining with a Doxford two-stroke and transfer to Hopemount ownership in 1932. *[Roy Fenton collection]*

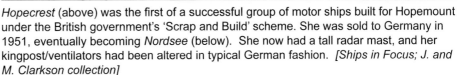

12. **HOPECREST** (2) 1935-1951
O.N. 161581 5,099g 3,106n 9,595d.
418.0 x 57.4 x 25.6 feet.
2SCSA 4-cyl. (23$^5/8$ x 91$^7/16$ inches)
oil engine by Barclay, Curle and Co.
Ltd., Glasgow; 222 NHP, 2,800 BHP,
12 knots.
18.3.1935: Launched by Barclay, Curle
and Co. Ltd., Glasgow (Yard No. 563).
25.4.1935: Registered in the ownership
of Hopemount Shipping Co. Ltd.
(A. Stott and Co. Ltd., managers),
Newcastle-upon-Tyne as HOPECREST.
5.1935: Completed.
20.9.1951: Register closed on sale to
Bugsier Reederei und Bergungs A.G.,
Hamburg, West Germany and renamed
FRIEDENAU.
19.10.1954: Sold to Wilh. Schuchmann
Reederei, Bremerhaven and renamed
NORDSEE.
3.7.1963: Arrived at Hamburg to be
broken up by Eisen und Metal A.G.

To be concluded.

Hopecrest (above) was the first of a successful group of motor ships built for Hopemount under the British government's 'Scrap and Build' scheme. She was sold to Germany in 1951, eventually becoming *Nordsee* (below). She now had a tall radar mast, and her kingpost/ventilators had been altered in typical German fashion. *[Ships in Focus; J. and M. Clarkson collection]*

FATE OF FEARLESS

In 1903 the Houston Line bought two short-sea vessels from the Cork Steam Ship Co. Ltd., *Dotterel* (1,402/1878) and *Ptarmigan* (1,234/1890). The new names given to them, *Fearless* and *Dauntless*, were quite out of keeping with the rest of the fleet of the British and South American Steam Navigation Co. Ltd. They were chosen to mark Houston's determination to fight the established Conference lines to gain a foothold in the South African trades in the aftermath of the Boer War. *Fearless* and *Dauntless* were acquired to run a feeder service between Liverpool and continental ports.

On the morning tide on 6th February 1906 *Fearless* set out from Liverpool for Hamburg with general cargo. In fog about three miles west of the North West Light Vessel she was hit by the Cardiff-registered steamer *Patricia* (843/1901). The latter was owned by Michael Murphy Ltd. of Dublin, and was herself outward bound with coal from Garston to Dublin. *Patricia* clouted *Fearless* just aft of her bridge, the collier sustaining damage to her bows above the waterline sufficient for her to return to Garston: that she could go back so far indicates she was in no great danger. *Fearless* was much more seriously wounded, and although she too could put back into the Mersey, she was beached off Egremont on the Wirral shore.

The Salvage Association attended *Fearless* almost immediately, but found that when the tide ebbed she had broken her back, as is clear from the photograph below which was probably taken on 7th February. The Salvage Association surveyor's list of damage was extensive, and

he reported she was 'too badly hogged for strapping'. He strongly advised the owners not to spend any money trying to save her. She was in fact almost immediately abandoned, and the Mersey Docks and Harbour Board took charge as was their statutory duty with what was considered a danger to navigation. Heavy weather caused further damage, and on 9th February a report in 'Lloyd's List' described cargo being washed out of *Fearless* and strewn along the beach between New Brighton and Egremont. In the photograph below, drums can be seen about to fall out of her hold.

Salvage of *Fearless* entailed finishing the work begun by *Patricia*, and cutting her in half. The fore part was refloated on 8th March and towed to Tranmere Beach, the after part following it on 19th March. John McRoberts reports her as being scrapped, but no details are known about who did the work. Perhaps it was those who had cut up the *Great Eastern*.

Subsequent proceedings in the Admiralty Division of the High Court found *Patricia* to blame, and her owners were held liable for a sum not exceeding £6,412 1s 7d, someone having made a remarkably precise calculation of losses.

After the loss of *Fearless* Houston's feeder service was discontinued, and in 1907 *Dauntless* was sold and renamed *Lapland*, later to be sunk as a blockship at Scapa. *Patricia* soldiered on with Murphy until 1912, and after a succession of owners in Antwerp, Newcastle-upon-Tyne, Belfast and Cardiff was wrecked early in 1924.

A few days later than the photograph opposite, the stern of *Fearless* has been cut away, dating these photographs off Tranmere to between 8th and 19th March 1906. Various boilers can be seen on her deck, presumably to drive pumps to remove water from the forepart of the hull to expedite refloating. The occupation of the gentleman on the ladder (right) is intriguing: is he repairing a rent in the hull?

Fearless was now 28 years old, having run out of Cork as *Dotterel* for 25 of those years. Owners, the Cork Steam Ship Co. Ltd., could trace their origins to the St. George Steam Packet Company of 1821. A restructuring of this company in 1843 saw the City of Cork Steam Ship Company take over its remaining services out of Cork, quickly restyled the Cork Steam Ship Company. In 1871 the City of Cork name was revived for the company's coastal services, its foreign lines continuing under the title Cork Steam Ship Co. Ltd. until 1927. The City of Cork name survived, as part of Coast Lines' operations, until 1965.

FEARLESS 1903-1906

O.N. 76865 1,422g 896n
264.8 x 32.1 x 21.8 feet
C. 2-cyl. by James Jack and Co., Liverpool; 150 NHP.
1888: Engine tripled by D. Rollo and Sons, Liverpool; 163 NHP.
8.1878: Launched by W.H. Potter and Son, Liverpool (Yard No. 80) for the Cork Steam Ship Co. Ltd., Cork as DOTTEREL.
26.10.1878: Registered.
5.11.1903: Acquired by the British and South American Steam Navigation Co. Ltd. (R.P. Houston and Co., managers), Liverpool.
12.11.1903: Renamed FEARLESS.
6.2.1906: Collided in fog with the steam ship PATRICIA about three miles west of the North West Light Vessel in Liverpool Bay whilst on a voyage from Liverpool to Hamburg with general cargo. Put back into the River Mersey and beached off

Egremont where she was cut in two.
8.3.1906: Forepart refloated and taken to Tranmere Beach.
19.3.1906: After part refloated and taken to Tranmere Beach.
Both sections were broken up.
21.6.1906: Register closed.

PATRICIA 1901-1912

O.N. 111037 843g 368n
208.8 x 30.1 x 12.8 feet
T. 3-cyl. by David Rowan and Co., Glasgow; 115 NHP, 800 IHP, 10.75 knots.
12.1901: Completed by Murdoch and Murray, Port Glasgow (Yard No. 184).
23.12.1901: Registered in the ownership of Michael Murphy, Dublin as PATRICIA.
9.8.1904: Manager became James Holland, Cardiff.
14.9.1905: Transferred to Michael Murphy Ltd. (Joseph O'Dowd, manager), Dublin.
8.1912: Sold to Agence Maritime Walford

(Société Anonyme), Antwerp, Belgium and renamed GENT.
21.11.1914: Registered in the ownership of George A. Connell and George W. Grace, Newcastle-upon-Tyne.
6.12.1914: Transferred to the Side Shipping Co. Ltd. (Connell and Grace Ltd., managers), Newcastle-upon-Tyne and renamed FELLSIDE.
13.3.1916: Sold to James W. Little, London and Daniel C. Kemp (Robert L. Kemp), Belfast
8.4.1920: Sold to William Robson, Benjamin Davies and Edward R. Lewis, Cardiff.
16.6.1920: Transferred to the Farley Steam Navigation Co. Ltd. (William Robson, manager), Cardiff.
8.1.1924: Wrecked in Hunts Bay whilst on a voyage from Bordeaux to Swansea with a cargo of pit props.
10.5.1924: Register closed.

HOG ISLAND THREE
Roy Fenton

Looking at the history of Headlam's *Barnby,* it became apparent that she was a significant ship: the first of the 110 cargo ships delivered from the Hog Island yard in Pennsylvania at the end of the First World War. Enquiring of Bill Schell whether he could supply a photograph of her under her original name *Quistconck*, he not only replied in the affirmative but also pointed out that two other 'Hog Islanders' had United Kingdom careers under commercial ownership. This is their story.

'Built by the mile'
Faced with the problem of deploying an army to fight a war three thousand miles across the Atlantic, in 1917 the United States of America needed ships and many of them. Growth and development of shipping and shipbuilding in the USA had not kept pace with the nation's industrial development, and both industries lagged behind those of Europe, and especially of Great Britain. To make matters worse, by 1917 existing shipbuilding capacity was largely occupied with orders for Britain, France and neutral countries. The US government's solution was threefold: requisition all the ships currently building for non-nationals, place orders for a series of standard ships with existing yards plus some in Japan and China, and finance a number of new shipyards to be run by commercial organisations as agencies of the government. All these activities were entrusted to the United States Shipping Board (USSB), who in turn set up the Emergency Fleet Corporation.

The most ambitious of four 'agency' shipyards was the Hog Island development of the American International Shipbuilding Corporation. The site consisted essentially of 900 acres of marshland just south of the junction of the Schuylkill and Delaware rivers in Pennsylvania; its attractions being its availability, its long water frontage and its proximity to existing industry and railroad facilities. The land had to be drained before work could begin on building 50 slips, 28 fitting out berths, the associated workshops, 82 miles of railroad track plus the small matter of houses and facilities for up to 30,000 workers. The work was not helped by the winter of 1917-1918 being one of the harshest that Philadelphia had ever experienced, and explosives had to be used to allow piles to be driven into the frozen ground. In putting it all together in the shortest possible time, the American International Shipbuilding Corporation had assistance from the New York Shipbuilding Corporation at Camden, New Jersey, a shipbuilder also owned by the same parent company, Stone and Webster of Boston.

This was not to be a conventional shipyard, with frames, plates and other hull parts largely manufactured on site. Instead it was a vast assembly plant, designed to put together components fabricated elsewhere, often many hundreds of miles from Pennsylvania. No component would be larger than could be accommodated on a standard US railroad flatcar, and curved plates were largely avoided: the hulls had no sheer or camber. Prefabrication meant that components had to be rigidly standardised, and with them the ships that were produced, this giving rise to the joke that the Hog Island ships were 'built by the mile and cut off by the yard'.

At least one US author has claimed that the Hog Island programme was the first time in history that ships were mass produced. However, Harland and Wolff had already designed the N type fabricated ship for the British government's shipbuilding programme, and - although not

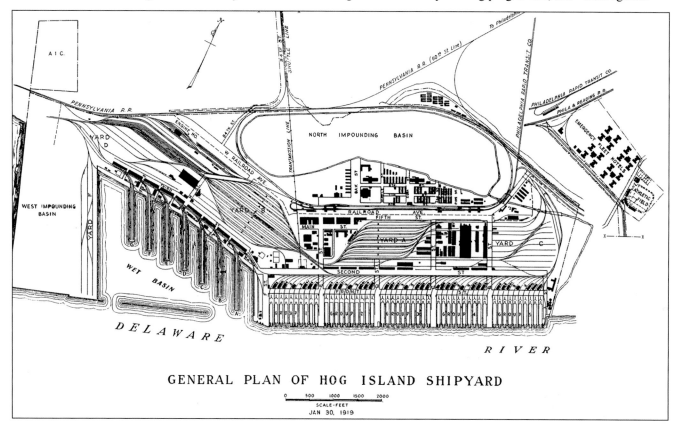

GENERAL PLAN OF HOG ISLAND SHIPYARD

on anything like the same scale as Hog Island - yards were especially laid out to build them in Britain, at Haverton Hill-on-Tees and at Chepstow. The initial N type was completed several months before the first US prefabricated example, the *War Climax* being delivered on 28th September 1918, albeit by an established yard, that of Swan, Hunter and Wigham Richardson Ltd. at Wallsend-on-Tyne.

Names and numbers

Prefabrication meant that, even before the Hog Island yard was fully completed, keels could be laid on the berths which were ready, the first on 16th February 1918. It was planned to construct two types of ships at the yard, the most numerous being a two-deck cargo ship propelled at 11 knots by steam turbines. The decision to disdain the single-deck, triple-expansion-engined tramp which made up a high proportion of the British First World War shipbuilding output reflected the very reasonable belief that, once the war was over, the USA would not be able to run such ships profitably. These cargo ships were given two titles, 'Emergency Fleet Corporation Design 1022', and 'Standard Fabricated Type A'. However, they became almost universally known as 'Hog Islanders', reflecting both their place of origin and their charmless appearance: in loaded condition, they indeed looked hogged. In September 1917 an initial order was placed for fifty of this type, although the received wisdom was that true economies of scale could only be achieved with numbers in excess of two hundred. In May 1918, well before any had been launched, a further sixty were ordered. All were to be completed. Eventually.

'Standard Fabricated Type B' was to be a troop transport, but a similar outlook to that which influenced the design of the 'A' type led to it being designed for a post-war role as a passenger-cargo ship. A total of seventy were ordered but, unlike the 'A' type, many were cancelled, and just twelve were delivered.

Names given to the 'A' type were a fascinating collection. The first hull was to be named *Red Jacket* in commemoration of the celebrated clipper of that name.

However, the First Lady, Edith Wilson, took an interest, and suggested that the ship should carry the native American name for the shipyard site, meaning 'place fit for hogs'. Her suggestion was adopted, and Mrs Wilson duly launched the ship as *Quistconck* on 5th August 1918. Many of the 'A' types went on to receive native American names, not all being quite as pronounceable as *Kishacoquillas* (yard number 519). Areas that had proved 'patriotic' in buying more than their expected quota of government war bonds were also celebrated, explaining the names of *City of Flint* (1510) and *Pipestone County* (532). *Schenectady* (511) presumably honoured the city in New York state where the General Electric Company made the turbines for Hog Islanders. The name *Liberty Bell* (1507) had particular resonance in Pennsylvania, and there must be stories behind the names *American Press* (1515), *Blue Triangle* (1512) and *Salvation Lass* (530), and the decision to yet again deny the name *Red Jacket*, intended for the first ship of the second order, and replace it with *Inspector* (1482).

The yard numbering scheme did not, as might be expected, start at 1 for the new yard. Instead, Emergency Fleet Corporation order numbers were adopted: 492 to 541 for the first batch ordered, and 1482 to 1541 for the remaining sixty 'A' types.

The Hog Island yard closed after its last ship was delivered in January 1921. In 1930 the land was sold to the City of Philadelphia, who initially used it for railroad purposes, and later built an airport on the site and developed a tanker terminal. Just a decade later the yard could have been the nucleus of another emergency shipbuilding programme.

Costs and corruption

When the Hog Island programme was being planned, cost does not appear to have been a major issue compared with the urgent need to produce ships for the war effort. The initial estimate for the programme was $27,000,000. By the time of the Armistice on 11th November 1918, only *Quistconck* had run trials, and even she was not delivered until December. With the war over, cost did become an issue, especially when

The first Hog Islander, *Quistconck* was photographed in the Cape Cod Canal on 22nd February 1940, probably running for Lykes Coastwise Line Inc. *[Eric Johnson collection/Bill Schell]*

it was revealed that – after the last ship had been delivered on 21st January 1921 – the final cost of the programme was £66,000,000, some 144% over budget. Worse, the glut of ships built during the war meant that, once the post-war boom in freight rates ended, the value of the Hog Islanders plummeted. Congress began to ask questions about the costs involved, and the hearings revealed that there had been widespread corruption, perhaps inevitably when huge amounts of government money were being thrown at projects, with little time or will to audit them adequately.

As early as June 1919 Hog Islanders began to be sold by the United States Shipping Board to commercial operators. However, as the Board was more than willing to let operators hire the vessels, often with encouragement to use them on government-sponsored routes, there was little incentive to buy them outright at asking prices of up to $215 per deadweight ton. Cautious private buyers were proved correct, as the Board had to take back a significant proportion of the ships it had sold, as freight rates and ship values tumbled and operators defaulted on payment. By 1928, when Congress ended the Emergency Fleet Corporation and belatedly demanded that government-owned ships be sold, prices had plummeted to as little as $5.75 per deadweight ton for a large batch sold to the Export Steamship Corporation.

Despite this gloomy picture, the Hog Islanders proved to be amongst the most commercially useful of the two thousand plus ships built for the Emergency Fleet Corporation. Relatively few were idle during the years between the wars, and many worked, as foreseen, as cargo liners on the routes of US owners. Lykes Lines had eight in their own name, acquiring another nine through various take-overs. Moore-McCormack and the Export Steamship Corporation each had fifteen Hog Island 'A' types, with four of the former company's ships being given more than adequate passenger accommodation for services to northern Europe. Less active were the six transferred to the US Navy in 1921, one of which, *Spica* (built as *Shannock*, yard number 527), spent eighteen years idle in reserve before going to war in 1940.

Tulsa was launched on 26th July 1919 when the daughter of a Tulsa oil man splashed crude oil from Oklahoma wells over the ship's bows. She was delivered on 20th September 1919, remaining with the United States Shipping Board until 1928 when, following a change of government policy, she was sold to the South Atlantic Steamship Co. Inc., in whose ownership she was photographed on 16th June 1934. Surviving the war, in 1946 she was sold to Argentina, this country, like Turkey, being able to afford only the least expensive ships. As *Formosa* she lasted until broken up at Buenos Aires in late 1960, Argentina and Brazil being amongst the last countries to operate Hog Islanders. *[Roy Fenton collection]*

By the Second World War, four Hog Island freighters had been lost and two broken up (one after being damaged). War service under the US flag for ships that were into their third decade seems to have been arduous, with assignment to Arctic convoys, for instance. In his detailed work 'The Hog Islanders', Goldberg records that a total of 41 were lost under US and other flags during the war. Casualties during wartime therefore accounted for about 40 per cent of the 'A' types extant in 1939.

Sold to the British government
Having run out of allies by mid-1940, the British looked across the North Atlantic to help make good its increasingly serious losses of merchant ships. In the midst of another programme to rejuvenate its own merchant fleet, largely neglected since the First World War, the United States government refused to allow Britain to place orders with existing shipyards. Undaunted, the British Shipbuilding Mission to North America ordered the sixty 10,000-ton 'Oceans' from yards in California and Maine which were yet to be built. This was an interesting echo of the Hog Island developments in 1917, and meant that, in paying for these yards, the British taxpayer was helping fund the future

Empire name	Yard No.	USSB name	Fate
Empire Falcon	492	*Quistconck*	See *Barnby*.
Empire Barracuda	494	*Sacandaga*	*15.12.1941*: Torpedoed by *U 77* west of Gibraltar.
Empire Ortolan	541	*Labette*	See *Stanland*.
Empire Hawk	1489	*Coahoma County*	*12.12.1942*: Sunk by *Enrico Tazzoli* off Brazil.
Empire Shearwater	1491	*Clearwater*	See *St. Jessica*.
Empire Mahseer	1507	*Liberty Bell*	*4.3.1943*: Torpedoed by *U 160* in the Indian Ocean.
Empire Razorbill	1521	*Conness Peak*	*1947*: Sold to Greek owners.
Empire Flamingo	1525	*Jolee*	*9.6.1944*: Sunk as part of Mulberry Harbour.
Empire Dolphin	1540	*Vaba*	*2.1947*: Broken up.

British ships visiting the neutral United States in the early years of the Second World War were routinely photographed by the United States Coastguard. This shot of the Hog Islander *Empire Ortolan* was taken on 28th May 1943. Unlike four of her British government-owned sisters which were either torpedoed or expended as breakwaters during the Second World War, she survived to become *Stanland*. *[David Whiteside collection]*

'Liberty' ship programme. It is only fair to point out that, without the immense war effort of the USA, those same Britishers might just have ended up being taxed, or worse, by the Third Reich.

The USA put no impediment in the way of Britain buying tonnage which had been built for the First World War. In 1940 and 1941 over one hundred ships were purchased by the British government direct from the United States Shipping Board or from private owners, although several of these failed to survive their delivery voyages. Amongst these were the nine Hog Island 'A' types listed opposite, all bought from commercial owners.

British commercial ownership

Of the nine which were bought by Britain, three were lost through enemy action, a proportion slightly lower than that for the full quota of U.S. ships bought in 1940 and 1941, about half of which were lost according to Mitchell and Sawyer's estimate. One British Hog Islander was sunk deliberately as a blockship in Normandy, and another was broken up whilst still in government ownership. Four passed to commercial owners, all initially British apart from *Empire*

Razorbill which became the Greek-owned *M. Xilas*, only to be burnt out and become a total loss within months.

The three British owners of Hog Islanders could hardly be more different from each other. First sold, but only by a matter of days, was *Empire Ortolan* which went to the Stanhope Steamship Co. Ltd. in July 1946. The company's manager, Jack Billmeir, had earned his money and reputation running the blockade of Spanish ports during the Civil War, and operated a post-war fleet which was almost unmatched in its variety. It included United States standard ships from both world wars, the latter comprising a 'Liberty', two T2 tankers and two turbine-engined 'Victory' types. The last named were quickly sold to P&O at a considerable profit.

It took Billmeir over a year to rename *Empire Ortolan* as *Stanland*, and even longer to appoint its first master, Captain H. Cutler, who joined her officially at Newport in December 1947. Given the chronic shortage of shipping post-war, it can only be assumed she was awaiting repairs all this time, and her not infrequent future breakdowns support this. She finally sailed from Swansea for Casablanca on 18th December 1947, returning to Middlesbrough in January. She then made three consecutive

Stanland discharging to lighters at Montevideo on 12th March 1948. She had arrived the previous day from Middlesbrough via Freetown, Sierra Leone, and sailed for Villa Constitucion on 15th March. *[Raul Maya/Bill Schell]*

Headlam's *Barnby*, photographed by C.R.V. Solomon, probably at Cape Town. *[Roy Fenton collection]*

round voyages to South America, calling on the way at Freetown, St. Vincent in the Cape Verde Islands or Madeira, presumably for bunkers. Apart from the first voyage, departure was from Barry or Newport, and in two cases the British port of arrival was Glasgow. The regularity suggests a charter to a liner company. Ports served in South America included Rio de Janeiro, Buenos Aires, Montevideo, Rio Grande and Rosario. None of these three voyages were trouble free with dynamo and boiler damage when arriving at Rio on the first, and machinery breakdown requiring a return to Buenos Aires on the second. On the third, a fire in the engine room in January 1949 delayed her at Glasgow for six weeks. This might have persuaded Billmeir to sell her, or her charterer to terminate her hire, as on the return voyage *Stanland* broke the pattern of the previous two voyages by calling homeward at Freetown, Pepel (presumably for iron ore), Dakar and Lisbon. Arriving back in Middlesbrough, she was sold to London-Greek owners.

Next to reach commercial ownership was *Empire Falcon*, formerly the pioneering *Quistconck*. New owners were the Rowland and Marwood's Steamship Co. Ltd. managed by Headlam and Son. In contrast to the relative newcomer Billmeir, Headlam was almost as venerable as their home port of Whitby. The company were adherents of the long-bridge-deck, triple-expansion-engined tramp right into the 1930s, and their acquisition of a steam-turbine-driven ship, built thirty years earlier across the Atlantic, must have been a surprise for observers. Under the name *Barnby*, she was the only one of the three ships which could be regarded as a tramp,

making eighteen round voyages, following no regular pattern of loading or discharge. The Voyage Record Cards give details of ports called at but not cargoes, and these need to be assumed from the voyage pattern. Ten voyages were to South or Central America, usually loading outwards at a British coal port, on the Tyne, in South Wales and once each at Grangemouth and Immingham. Destinations included ports in Brazil, Uruguay, Argentina and Cuba. The return trip probably carried grain, calling at Falmouth (for orders?) then proceeding to a variety of ports, including Burntisland, Dundee and Grangemouth. Six voyages were made to the Mediterranean, again probably loading coal outwards, at the ports mentioned earlier, or on one occasion at Partington on the Manchester Ship Canal. The coal went to Italian ports, from where *Barnby* dropped back to a North African port – Sfax, Bougie or Casablanca – to load phosphate or possibly esparto grass. The remaining two voyages to West Africa are more difficult to fathom out, as the destination was Takoradi and on both occasions the British terminal

Mariandrea, formerly *Barnby,* photographed in London. She made just one visit to this port, between 10th and 24th May 1952. *[Alex Duncan/Bill Schell]*

port was Middlesbrough, suggesting that the cargo was iron ore. During her voyages *Barnby* had recurring problems with defective boilers or turbines. The most serious was in January 1949 when, having left the Tyne for Central America on New Year's Day, *Barnby* put back into Falmouth after four days with a defective turbine, was towed to Plymouth for repair, set out again on 18th January, only to put back into Falmouth again on January 24th, further repairs taking two months, but at last solving her problems.

The last of the three Hog Islanders to remain in British ownership, on 14th January 1952 *Barnby* arrived from Bougie at Liverpool, where she was sold to Italian owners, who put her under the Panama flag as *Mariandrea*. There was only limited life left in the 33-year-old veteran, her new owners first sending her to Narvik to load ore for Antwerp. Loading in London (where the accompanying photograph was taken), she then worked her way slowly out east via Suez, making a series of relatively short voyages in the Indian Ocean, before returning to the Mediterranean. Here she loaded a final cargo of iron ore at Bona which she delivered to Barrow-in-Furness on 20th February 1953, where she was sold for scrap. Although several Hog Islanders were broken up by Wards at Barrow, *Mariandrea* went to breakers in Troon, arriving in early March.

Last of the three Hog Islanders to leave Ministry ownership was the *Empire Shearwater*. Richard Street, founder of the South American Saint Line, was anxious to resume services from the United Kingdom and Antwerp as quickly as possible, and bought a number of second-hand ships whilst placing orders for new cargo liners. The contrast between *St. Jessica*, as the Hog Islander was renamed, and the *St. Essylt* launched at Sunderland in September 1947 could not be more stark. The new ship, first of four, was fast, sleek, streamlined and praised for the high standard of her crew accommodation. Her

fifteen-knot service speed contrasted with the nine knots that surveyors had reckoned to be the best that the Hog Islander could manage when she came under British registration in August 1940.

Taken over in London in August 1946, *St. Jessica* sailed from Liverpool in September, calling at Hull and Antwerp before proceeding to South America via Las Palmas. She made a total of five round voyages to South America, her usual European ports being Hull and Antwerp (with London and Cardiff recording one visit each). Those in South America were Rio de Janeiro, Buenos Aires, Rosario, Montevideo and on one occasion San Lorenzo. Bunkering stops were usually made at Teneriffe or Las Palmas. Breakdowns reported were much rarer than with *Stanland* and *Barnby*, helping *St. Jessica* to complete her five South American voyages in 18 months.

Her next two voyages are more difficult to explain for a ship operated by the South American Saint Line. Her fifth voyage terminated at Burntisland, where she spent ten days presumably discharging a cargo loaded over four days in Takoradi. After a brief call at London she proceeded to

Above: The svelte *St. Essylt*. [B. and A. Fielden/J. and M. Clarkson]
Below: *St Jessica* makes a smoky departure from Cape Town, a port she visited just twice, dating this photo to either 19th July or 11th October 1949. Comparing this photograph with those of *Barnby*, *Stanland* and other Hog Islanders, reveals that *St Jessica's* bridge had been extensively rebuilt. [Ships in Focus]

Port Elizabeth and other ports in south and east Africa. Homeward she visited Barcelona, Hamburg and Bremen before returning to Hull and Antwerp. Her eighth and final voyage as *St. Jessica* took her back to Africa, with calls at Cape Town, Port Elizabeth, Durban, Beira, Mombasa (where a leak was discovered in a hold), Mocambique, Lourenço Marques, Cape Town, Luderitz, Walvis Bay and Lobito. A return to Bremen via Antwerp and Rotterdam might suggest a charter to a German line. Brief calls were then made at four Danish ports before she arrived at Hull on 22nd December 1949 only to be sold to Turkish owners.

Last rites

The one-time *St. Jessica* lasted as *Karsiyaka* under Turkish ownership until 1959, and three other Hog Islanders also worked for Turks into the 1950s: *Atlantik* (the former *Luxpalile*, yard number 529), *Huseyin Kapitan* (ex-*Saugerties*, yard number 507), and *Demirhan* (ex-*Saco*, yard number 496). But were these the last of the class? It turned out that the Turks had been survived by Japanese, Soviet and South American examples. *Riga*, originally *Blair* yard number 516, and one of several Hog Islanders supplied under Lend-Lease to the USSR who had simply omitted to return them, was withdrawn in 1961, but the date of her demolition is not known. The Argentinean *Pleamar* (ex-*Shannock*, yard number 527) was broken up in 1964. She may well have been the last of the Hog Islanders in more-or-less original condition, although the US Navy had equipped her as an armed transport during the Second World War. Another late survivor had been converted to a crab cannery in 1955, the Japanese *Tokei Maru* (originally *Schroon*, yard number 515) which sank off Luzon on 3rd November 1965 after catching fire.

Almost certainly the last Hog Island 'A' type hull to remain above water was the former *Schenectady*, yard number 511. She was by no means standard, as in 1932 she had been fitted with by all accounts excellent accommodation for 90 passengers and as *Scanyork* placed on services to Scandinavia and the Baltic. Replaced by C2-types in 1940, she and three sisters were sold by Moore McCormack to Brazil in order to operate between Rio and New York. As *Maua*, Lloyd Brasiliero disposed of her to breakers in 1964, but she remained laid up at Rio Janeiro, where she was last reported in August 1967. She had lasted for at least 48 years, justifying the trust the United States Shipping Board had in the design it ordered in unprecedented numbers in 1917.

Luxpalile (yard number 529) was one of no fewer than five Hog Island freighters launched on Memorial Day, 30th May 1919. After a US career under several names, she was sold to Turkey in 1949 as *Sadikli* being renamed *Atlantik* a year later. She is seen (top) on 8th June 1953 shortly after her arrival at Barrow with a cargo of iron ore, and, after discharge, waiting to be broken up there by Thos. W. Ward Ltd. (bottom). How times change: with Aliaga in Turkey one of the world's major centres of shipbreaking, it is inconceivable that a Turkish ship would be sent to the United Kingdom for demolition. *[Ken Royall collection]*

Hog Islanders in British commercial ownership

STANLAND 1946-1949
O.N. 168160 5,409g 3,291n.
390.0 x 54.2 x 27.6 feet.
Steam turbine by the General Electric Company, Schenectady, New York, U.S.A., 2,500 S.H.P., 10½ knots.
27.12.1918: Keel laid.
30.7.1919: Launched by the American International Shipbuilding Corporation, Hog Island, Pennsylvania, U.S.A. (Yard No. 541) for the United States Shipping Board, Washington D.C., U.S.A. as LABETTE.
24.9.1919: Delivered.
1937: Sold to Lykes Brothers - Ripley Steam Ship Co. Inc., New Orleans, U.S.A.
1937: Transferred to Lykes Coastwise Line Inc., Houston, U.S.A.
28.4.1941: Registered in the ownership of the Ministry of Shipping (J.A. Billmeir and Co., Ltd., managers), London as EMPIRE ORTOLAN.
1.5.1941: Owners became the Ministry of War Transport, London.
2.7.1946: Owners became the Ministry of Transport, London.
3.7.1946: Sold to Stanhope Steamship Co. Ltd. (J.A. Billmeir and Co. Ltd., managers), London.
31.7.1947: Renamed STANLAND.
27.10.1949: Register closed on sale to Alma Shipping Co. S.A., Panama (John Frangos and Mrs. Anna Frango) (Faros Shipping Co. Ltd., London, managers) and renamed ALMA.
31.3.1953: Arrived at Milford Haven to be broken up by T.W. Ward Ltd.

BARNBY 1946-1952
O.N. 168079 5,494g 3,264n.
390.0 x 54.2 x 27.9 feet.
Steam turbine by the General Electric Company, Schenectady, New York, U.S.A.; 2,500 SHP, 10½ knots.
5.8.1918: Launched by the American International Shipbuilding Corporation, Hog Island, Pennsylvania, U.S.A. (Yard No. 492) for the United States Shipping Board, Washington D.C., U.S.A. as QUISTCONCK.
7.11.1918: Ran trials.
3.12.1918: Delivered.
3.1.1919: Sailed from Norfolk, Virginia on maiden voyage to Colon, Panama.
1933: Sold to Lykes Brothers - Ripley Steam Ship Co. Inc., New Orleans, U.S.A.
1937: Transferred to Lykes Coastwise Line Inc., Houston, U.S.A.

Empire Ortolan at Halifax, Nova Scotia, Canada. *[National Maritime Museum, P22404]*

A further photograph of *Barnby* illustrates how a well-laden Hog Islander could appear hogged. *[Ships in Focus]*

95

11.3.1941: Registered in the ownership of the Ministry of Shipping, London (Headlam and Son, Whitby, managers) as EMPIRE FALCON.
1.5.1941: Owners became the Ministry of War Transport, London.
8.4.1946: Owners became the Ministry of Transport, London.
30.7.1946: Sold to Rowland and Marwood's Steamship Co. Ltd. (Headlam and Son), Whitby.
4.11.1946: Renamed BARNBY.
2.2.1952: Register closed on sale to Sociedad de Navegacion Magliveras S.A., Panama (Luigi Monta fu Carlo, Genoa, Italy) and renamed MARIANDREA.
3.3.1953: Arrived Troon to be broken up by the West of Scotland Shipbreaking Co. Ltd.

ST. JESSICA 1946-1950
O.N. 167632 4,970g 3,046n.
390.0 x 54.2 x 27.8 feet.
Steam turbine by the General Electric Company, Schenectady, New York, U.S.A.; 2,500 SHP, 9 knots.
15.1.1920: Launched by the American International Shipbuilding Corporation, Hog Island, Pennsylvania, U.S.A. (Yard No. 1491) for the United States Shipping Board, Washington D.C., U.S.A. as CLEARWATER.
8.3.1920: Delivered.
1929: Sold to the Mississippi Shipping Co. Inc. (Delta Line), New Orleans, U.S.A.
21.8.1940: Registered in the ownership of the Ministry of Shipping, London

The *Karsiyaka* formerly the *St Jessica*. Part of her previous name can still be seen. *[J. and M. Clarkson collection]*

(Douglas and Ramsey, Glasgow, managers), as EMPIRE SHEARWATER.
1.5.1941: Owners became the Ministry of War Transport, London.
1946: Owners became the Ministry of Transport, London.
27.8.1946: Sold to St. Quentin Shipping Co. Ltd., Newport, Monmouthshire.
5.9.1946: Renamed ST. JESSICA.
16.1.1950: Register closed on sale to Avni Nuri Meserretcioglu, Izmir, Turkey

and renamed KARSIYAKA.
2.1958: Laid up at Istanbul.
5.6.1959: Breaking up began at Istanbul - Kalafatyeri with unrepaired stranding damage sustained in January 1958.

Note: the transfer of official ownership from the Ministry of Shipping to the Ministry of War Transport on 1st May 1941 is not recorded in the three ships' registration documents.

Empire Dolphin remained in Government ownership after the war until she was sold for breaking up, arriving at the Briton Ferry yard of Thos. W. Ward Ltd. on 23rd February 1947. Completed as the *Vaba* she had been converted into a tanker in 1923 and appears to have served as such to the end of her career. This is supported by the fact that she was managed by the tanker owners Gow, Harrison and Co. for the Ministry of War Transport. *[National Maritime Museum, P22277]*

THE FRENCH BOUNTY SHIP BOOM 1897-1902
Part 1
John Naylon

For the British sailing ship historian the curtain call for the big deep-water sailing vessel – the Cape Horner – is usually associated with the surge in United Kingdom construction in the late 1880s and early 1890s – a response to the huge growth of Britain's steam tramp fleet. The advent of Siemens-Martin steel - lighter, cheaper yet of high quality - from 1885 onwards allowed the production of stronger, high-pressure, marine boilers, which facilitated the development of the triple-expansion engine. The efficiency of the triple-expansion engine reduced coal consumption by 60 per cent and by the end of the 1880s steam tramps could travel at nine knots on a fuel consumption of only half an ounce of coal per ton-mile. Steamers became as economical to operate as sailing vessels and, although the latter could be built for half the cost of steamers, the steamer could compensate by making three voyages to the sailing ship's one, earning as much as four times more per year and double the annual return on investment. Steam tramps could now compete with sail worldwide.

This challenge stimulated the building of very large iron and steel full riggers and barques, especially during the years 1888 to 1892, when 465 big square riggers left British yards. The new Siemens-Martin process was of course also available to sailing ship constructors and also, for a while, sail retained an advantage over steam in certain long-haul bulk trades in which seasonality of production, coupled with loading inconveniences and delays, made steam ship operation uneconomic. The British sailing ship building boom peaked in 1891 (139 launchings) and 1892 (143); this latter year was also the last (except for the anomaly of 1920, experiencing the effects of the First World War) in which the world's sail tonnage increased over the previous year's. About 70 per cent of all deep-water sailing vessels launched in 1892 were British-built.

Decline rapidly followed. In 1893 British launchings dropped to 69, in 1894 to 42, and thereafter fell away and faded out in the first decade of the twentieth century. Trading opportunities for sail continued to dwindle, bringing

Caroline was a British-built barque acquired and renamed by A.-D. Bordes of Dunkirk in 1909. Builders as *Muskoka* were Richardson, Duck and Company at Stockton-on-Tees in 1891, the peak year for sailing ship construction in the United Kingdom. Her owners were originally based in Windsor, Nova Scotia, although she was re-registered in London in 1902. A post-war sale to Compagnie Française d'Armement et d'Importation de Nitrate de Soude was short-lived: whilst running between Coronel and Antofagasta with coal *Caroline* was beached, on fire, near the latter port on 19th July 1920. *[Author's collection]*

diminishing or uncertain profits and longer stays in port and periods of inactivity, and sailing ship operation gradually became a marginal and precarious activity, sensitive to even modest movements in freight rates. These were squeezed during much of the 1890s and, although rates rose again from 1897 onwards as a consequence of the Spanish-American and Boer wars, in that same year there was a sharp increase in London insurance costs for sailing ships leading to a collapse in the market for new sail tonnage. These circumstances helped to confirm the correctness of most British owners' decision that the future lay in steam, and the United Kingdom exodus from sail can effectively be dated to 1897.

In contrast to this negative scenario, however, on the other side of the Channel a sailing ship boom was taking place, albeit prompted by different considerations and producing one of the biggest and most distinctive contributions to the last days of sail.

The nineteenth-century French merchant marine crisis

Since the time of Finance Minister Colbert in the seventeenth century, the French merchant marine, burdened with taxes and duties, had found it almost impossible to compete commercially with other maritime nations. The remedy had been state protection – the *surtaxe de pavillon* (flag surtax), first promulgated in 1793 and re-imposed in 1840, whereby cargo imports were penalised which were not carried under the *tricolore* or the flag of the country where the cargo originated. By the 1860s France was virtually the only country not to have gone over to free trade, despite continuous pressure from Britain. However, on 23rd January 1860 the Emperor Napoléon III, without reference to Parliament, signed a free-trade commercial treaty with the United Kingdom, and on 19th May 1866 the French Assembly abolished the *surtaxe de pavillon*.

This belated introduction of free trade had a disastrous effect upon

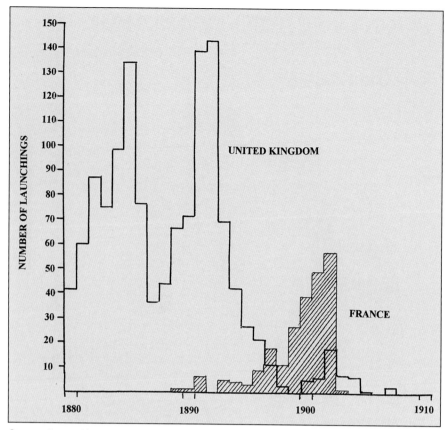

Comparison of launches of sailing vessels in the United Kingdom and France.

Bureau Veritas reported that the total number of sailing ships registered in France in that year was 3,877, with a total tonnage of 751,900, compared with 19,709 vessels in Britain totalling 5,543,600 tons. On 20th March 1872 a new subsidy law attempted to remedy the situation, but it was thwarted by previous treaties and agreements, which also prevented the reintroduction of the *surtaxe de pavillon*.

The 1881 subsidy law

In 1880 70 per cent of French overseas trade was still being carried under foreign flags. In keeping with the French tradition of protectionism, the solution to the crisis was obviously a reversion to some form of state assistance. Accordingly, after six years of wrangling, a new measure was introduced by Dupuy de Lôme to support French shipbuilding and operation. The *Loi de prime* ('bounty law') of 29th January 1881 offered a cash allowance of 60 francs per gross ton to offset the cost of building iron and steel vessels (sail and steam) in France, plus a further operating bounty for sailing vessels engaged in foreign trade of 1.50 francs per net registered ton and per 1,000 miles travelled. The law was to last for ten years, the operating allowance falling by 5 centimes per year. Vessels built abroad for French owners and bought before 1st January 1891 attracted half the subsidy.

In practice, this compensatory legislation did little to encourage French shipping. Construction costs remained almost double those on the Clyde and only eight large, metal-hulled, sailing

French deep-water shipping. The industry was in any event disadvantaged compared with Britain due to the backward and stagnant state of French shipbuilding, still mainly using wood. In 1866 France possessed only ten iron sailing vessels. Most yards were small, lacked suitable management experience and qualified labour for a transition to metal hulls, and were unable to attract the capital needed for such a transition. While the evident answer for the French merchant fleet was modernisation, French-built iron (and later steel) vessels were bound to be significantly more expensive than their foreign competitors (one-third more costly compared with Britain). The marine engineer and designer Dupuy de Lôme calculated that the 1866 law gave an advantage of 40 francs per registered ton to foreign builders. The French iron and steel centres (Alsace, Lorraine, the Central Massif), unlike those of Britain, were distant from the Atlantic and Mediterranean coasts, while imports of building materials – especially metal plate for hulls and spars – were subject to customs duties of 75 gold francs per ton.

Accordingly, while technical and commercial arguments favoured metal hulls over wood, France lacked the cost advantages of Britain in construction and sales prices, and the problem was where to find the capital

for modernisation when sailing ship owners were working at a loss and were unable to attract investors or credit because of the poor prospects of returns. French ports, hitherto the monopoly of the *tricolore*, were now invaded by foreign vessels. Freight rate competition meant that by 1870 French ships were carrying only 27 per cent of national trade, and French wooden vessels were increasingly confined to such relatively short routes as to the West Indies and the eastern coasts of North and South America. In 1875

Built in 1871 well before the first subsidy law, the 596 gross ton wooden barque *Charles* of Granville gets underway from Le Havre. *[Author's collection]*

vessels were built in French yards between 1881 and 1891. Others were bought from abroad – especially from Britain – but only by such substantial owners as Antoine-Dominique Bordes et Fils. Results were equally disappointing for sailing ship owners. Operating costs were affected by declining freight rates after 1886, by the success of the Suez Canal (which sailing vessels could not use) and by competition from cheaply-built British steam tramps; and, not surprisingly, investors were hesitant to come forward. In 1886 the deep-sea sailing tonnage of the French merchant fleet was languishing in eighth place behind the United Kingdom, the United States, the British possessions, Norway, Germany, Italy and Sweden, at barely 400,000 net registered tons (mostly wood and composite) compared with the United Kingdom's 3.25 million tons (largely iron and steel). By 1891 the picture had improved to 1,157 vessels totalling 520,000 tons, compared with 735 vessels totalling 325,000 tons ten years earlier; but this still placed France just above Greece. In the words of the maritime historian Louis Lacroix, 'Only artificial and energetic measures could cure the sickness which stared our merchant marine in the face'.

Success at last: the 1893 subsidy law

This second subsidy law – the *Loi de prime à la navigation* of 30th January 1893 – was eventually to prove spectacularly effective. It substantially increased benefits so that the building subsidy rose from 60 to 65 francs per gross ton for iron or steel vessels, 40 francs for wooden ships and 150 for machinery (the *prime* was also paid for steamers). The operating subsidy was again calculated per one thousand miles travelled but was now based on gross instead of net tonnage and distinguished between sailing vessels (1.70 francs per ton) and steamers (1.10 francs). The *prime* was again to last for ten years, decreasing by one tenth each year, but now with the additional benefit of applying for this length of time to any new vessels built in a French yard in any year during the law's operation (i.e., for the first ten years of a vessel's life). The full *prime* was earned by vessels trading beyond 30 degrees south and 72 degrees north, and 15 degrees west and 44 degrees east of Paris; vessels trading foreign within those limits (whimsically described as the 'international coasting trade') received

Delivered in September 1882, *Union* was one of several four-masted, full-rigged ships ordered by Bordes et fils in response to the 1881 bounty law, builder being Russell and Company, Greenock. Still with Bordes over thirty years later, she was captured and scuttled by the *Kronprinz Wilhelm* in November 1914, after part of her cargo of South Wales coal destined for Valparaiso had been unloaded into the German auxiliary cruiser. *[Author's collection]*

Built by Alexander Stephen and Sons at Dundee in 1892, the iron and steel four-masted barque *Melita* was bought by Bordes et fils in 1894 and renamed *Marthe*. She was to have a relatively short life. On 10th May 1898 she arrived at her home port of Dunkirk from Pisagua with nitrate, but whilst being towed into the harbour in fog touched Ruytingen Bank. Attempts to refloat her failed and the next day she sprang a leak, capsized and sank, fortunately without loss of life. *[Author's collection]*

two-thirds of the rate. The half bounty for ships built abroad for French owners ceased to be operative. A subsidy of 15 francs per 100 kilos was also paid for the installation of labour-saving machinery in sailing ships, such as donkey boilers to provide steam for capstans, pumps and winches and Jarvis brace winches, built under licence by Le Sauvage et Patras of Le Havre (albeit with very little, if any, benefit to Captain Jarvis himself). Although the *prime* was also available for steamships

(indeed, over the years from 1893 to 1914, 19,966,000 francs went to steamers as compared with 21,131,000 francs paid to sailing vessels), much of the 1893 legislation was clearly designed to foster the creation of a new fleet of large, steel, deep-water, sailing ships to rival those of the United Kingdom. In this the 1893 law was eminently successful and the remainder of this article concerns itself with the big French Cape Horners qualifying for the full bounty.

It is interesting to note that Jules Siegfried, the Minister of Commerce who introduced the 1893 law, was deputy for the coastal *département* of Seine Inférieure and also, together with his brother Jacques, a principal shareholder in the Compagnie Havraise de Navigation à Voiles (also known as the Compagnie Édouard Corblet), founded in 1894, and the Compagnie des Voiliers Havrais (also known as the Compagnie Henri Génestal) founded in 1898, both of Le Havre.

There were no immediate results from the 1893 law. The French shipping industry was slow to respond to the increased bounties, partly because of a lack of investment capital but mainly due to the slump in freight rates from 1892 onwards. As we have seen, sailing ship construction, ownership and management was sensitive to the slightest shift in the economic environment. Partly because of the abundant tonnage being offered by British sailing vessels, freights for coal from Europe to Chile fell from 24 shillings per ton in 1888-1891 to 13 shillings after 1892, and return freights with nitrate from 34 to 23 shillings. After this dull start, however, rates began to rise again in 1897, finally touching off a French sailing ship construction boom which lasted for five years and more than doubled the net tonnage of the French deep-water sailing fleet, from 199,000 in 1896 to 468,000 in 1903.

From 1897 to 1902 French sailing shipbuilders and owners experienced unparalleled prosperity, at a time when steam appeared to be threatening the very life of the wind ship and British owners were ridding themselves of their fleets. France became one of the last countries to possess a significant sailing merchant marine and her deep-water sailers could now return to the long-haul trades hitherto in the hands, mainly, of the British: North American and Australian grain, Peruvian guano, Chilean nitrate, American case oil, New Caledonian nickel ore, British and Australian coal, and North American timber.

A range of figures testifies to the transformation – although the statistics vary according to source and criteria. During the operation of the 1893 law some 218 splendid steel square riggers entered the French merchant navy. By 1900 the total sailing fleet substantially outnumbered the steam fleet (French steam ship construction was actually declining) and by 1902 France was second only to the United Kingdom in sailing ship tonnage, albeit still a long way behind. Ulrich Schaefer gives some precise figures for deep-water vessels of over 1,000 tons: in 1898 France possessed 70 such vessels, totalling 118,913 registered tons, compared with Britain's 938 vessels registering

The *Presidente Félix Faure* was built in 1896 by Forges et Chantier de la Méditerranée, Le Havre for Compagnie Havraise de Navigation à Voiles, managed by Brown and Corblet of Le Havre who specialised in the New Caledonia nickel ore trade. She is said to have been modelled on the British four-masted barque *Marion Lightbody* (2,176/1888). One of only two bounty ships to carry skysails, the *Presidente Félix Faure* is credited with frequently logging 15 knots and running as much as 340 miles in a day. She made a passage from Le Havre to Noumea, New Caledonia in just 77 days.

She demonstrates that not all of the bounty ships carried elaborate and protective superstructures, but her long open deck made her vulnerable to a boarding sea. Her crew paid the price for this off the Kerguelen Islands on 2nd February 1898 when an entire watch of fifteen men was washed overboard when she was swept from stem to stern.

The 2,860 gross ton four-masted barque was wrecked on one of the Antipodes Islands on 13th March 1908 whilst carrying nickel ore from Pouembout in New Caledonia to Le Havre.

In 1899 the president after whom the barque was named died in office, quite literally. It was in his office in the Elysée Palace, where he was making love to his mistress. *[Author's collection]*

1,574,132 tons; by 1903 the French tally had risen to 207 vessels registering 356,557 tons, while the British figures had fallen to 700 ships and 1,201,490 tons. An article in the French journal 'L'Illustration' of 1910 ('Décadence de la Marine Marchande à Voile') offers a comparison of the proportion of sailing vessels in the British and French merchant fleets, which demonstrates the influence of the bounty system in the latter case. In Britain the percentage fell from 41 in 1888 to 12.6 in 1908 while in France it remained much the same – 47.9 in 1888 and 47.2 in 1908.

In 1902, the last year of the 1893 bounty, France built 57 deep-water steel sailing vessels totalling nearly 156,000 gross tons, compared with Britain's 17 vessels totalling 40,446 gross tons. The net tonnage of sailing vessels under the *tricolore* had increased from 199,000 in 1896 to 468,000 in 1903.

A shipbuilding frenzy

From 1897 onwards French building yards were inundated with orders and responded rapidly, often offering standard series of vessels to gain time. Existing yards modernised and new yards came into being, all working at full capacity. Nantes predominated in this frantic activity, turning out 123 three- and four-masted square riggers in less than fifty months and accounting for 60 per cent of all the new bounty ships launched. Especially prominent were Ateliers et Chantiers de la Loire, founded in 1881 and traditionally mainly involved with naval vessels and merchant steamers. Although sailing ships were only a minor part of their production, in 1897 they began the construction of standard models, mostly of 2,000-3,000 gross tons, and launched 67 vessels by 1902. Another big Nantes builder, Chantiers Dubigeon of Chantenay-sur-Loire founded in 1889, also began standard series construction in 1897, producing 28 ships. Perhaps the most remarkable offspring of the 1893 bounty law, however, were the builders Chantiers Nantais de Constructions Maritimes, also of Chantenay. Created to take up orders which other yards could not accept, in a short life of only 23 months (1900-1902) they launched 32 identical three-masted barques of 2,200 gross tons – prompting the belief (unsubstantiated as far as this author is aware) that the hulls were fabricated in Britain and

Cassard is manoeuvred against the quay at Hotwells prior to entering Bristol's Floating Harbour. The 2,289 gross ton barque was built in 1899 by the prolific Ateliers et Chantiers de la Loire at Saint Nazaire. Founded in 1891, coinciding with the first subsidy law, this yard built 79 deep-water sailing vessels with a total tonnage of 184,600. Of these, 69 were series-built vessels. Even so, sailing vessels were a relative minor part of the yard's output, which was dominated by warships and steam merchant ships.

On her maiden voyage from Nantes and Swansea to San Francisco, returning to Antwerp, *Cassard* returned a profit of 20.96 per cent for owners, Société des Armateurs Nantais. *Cassard* was lost on Bleaker Island in the Falklands on 20th May 1906 bound from Sydney to Europe with wheat. *[Author's collection]*

Dubigeon completed the 2,063 gross tons barque *Anne de Bretagne* at Nantes in April 1901 for Société Bretonne de Navigation, Rouen. *Anne de Bretagne* was captured and sunk by the German auxiliary cruiser *Kronprinz Wilhelm* in the Atlantic on 21st November 1914 whilst on a voyage from Fredrikstad to Melbourne with lumber. She was owned by Société Nouvelle d'Armement, Nantes at the time of her loss. *[Author's collection]*

shipped 'knocked-down' across the Channel for assembly in France.

The 1893 *prime* was therefore a godsend to French builders, since at the turn of the century construction costs in France were some 1.85 times greater than in the United Kingdom.

The bounty fleets

Over sixty ship owning companies and individual owners responded enthusiastically to the new optimism. Some were old-established companies, such as Antoine-Dominique Bordes et Fils, which commissioned 30 ships, while most companies came into existence (some as late as 1900) simply to take advantage of the *prime* and rising freight rates. It is difficult to be specific about the number of ship owners since some changed their names, merged or were just managers of others' vessels (Prentout-Leblond, Leroux et Compagnie of Rouen, for instance, managed several companies' ships as well as operating their own). This hectic and time-limited activity also attracted foreign investment. R.C. Rickmers of Bremerhaven became a director of the Compagnie Maritime Française and Léon Blum, a ship chandler of San Francisco, became a major shareholder in the Société Anonyme les Voiliers de Saint Nazaire – his investments being rewarded by the naming of the full-riggers *Léon Blum* and *Helène Blum* (after his wife).

Some companies specialised in particular trades. A-D. Bordes dominated the west coast of South America nitrate trade. The Californian grain trade saw the ships of the Société Bretonne de Navigation, the Société des Voiliers Français and the Société des Voiliers Dunkerquois. Prentout-Leblond specialized in bulk oil transport; while the New Caledonian nickel ore trade was largely in the hands of Brown et Corblet and the Compagnie des Voiliers Havrais.

As with shipbuilding, Nantes was confirmed as the home of the latter-day French Cape Horners. Of the 232 bounty ships

Guéthary was built in 1901 by the short-lived but highly productive yard of Chantiers Nantais de Constructions Maritimes for a Bayonne owner. The 2,297 gross ton barque was wrecked on 21st October 1914 near Ardmore Light, Islay nearing the end of a long voyage from Tchio, New Caledonia to Glasgow with nickel ore. At the time she was with Société Anonyme des Voiliers Normands, managed along with ships of several other companies by Prentout-Leblond, Leroux of Rouen. *[Author's collection]*

Léon Blum was built in 1902 for Ateliers et Chantiers de Normandie, Rouen for Société Anonyme les Voiliers de Saint Nazaire, in whom San Francisco ship chandler Léon Blum was an investor. Like so many bounty barques, she failed to survive the First World War, but was a victim of marine hazards rather than war, wrecked off Dakar when arriving with a grain cargo from Australia on 21st November 1917. She had been bought by Société Générale d'Armement of Nantes just prior to her loss. *[Author's collection]*

launched in France under the 1881 and 1893 laws, 122 were owned in Nantes (52.5%); and of the last generation of sailing ship companies at least 23 (and possibly 33) were registered there, including such substantial owners as the Compagnie Maritime Française (with 16 ships), the Société des Voiliers Nantois (14) and Compagnie de Navigation Française (12). These fleets, however, dwindled in comparison with those of Antoine-Dominique Bordes of Dunkirk and later Paris (42 ships already in 1883; 33 in 1905), Prentout-Leblond, in association with Henri Boniface, of Rouen (41) and the Société Generale d'Armement of Nantes, which came to outnumber them both. These three were the biggest sailing ship companies in the world.

Design of the bounty ships

It is interesting to compare the hull designs of the French bounty ships with those of their British contemporaries. The classic British profile was elegant but at the same time utilitarian: a long open main deck carrying one or two deckhouses for the crew, apprentices and galley; a short raised forecastle head and poop; minimum and basic accommodation for officers and crew; and dangerous working conditions, with the open main deck liable to be swept from end to end by boarding seas, sometimes with disastrous consequences.

By contrast, the terms of the *prime* directly influenced the design of many of the '1893' French Cape Horners. The payment of the bounty on gross tonnage covered non-cargo superstructures, encouraging builders to create unusually long poops and forecastles (though not, curiously, German-style midships bridges), providing dry and commodious accommodation (including separate mess rooms for the crew, something unheard of in British vessels) and donkey-engine rooms, and much greater security for work on deck while at the same time reducing the net tonnage upon which charges were based. These extensive superstructures, amounting sometimes to almost continuous upper decks, made the bounty ships immediately recognisable – especially if accompanied, as in the case of Bordes' vessels, by the line of painted ports along their bulwarks. The results were some of the most handsome and distinctive of latter-day square riggers, incorporating the latest developments for this type of vessel.

The bounty ships' rigs

We have been given the general impression that the last years of sail were dominated by the four-masted barque – an impression perhaps reinforced by the fact that most

Owned like so many later bounty ships in Nantes, *Desaix* was built in 1902 by Chantiers et Atelier de Saint Nazaire for Compagnie Maritime Française. Changing hands several times, the 2,391 gross ton ship was with Société Générale d'Armement when broken up late in 1927. *[Author's collection]*

Built in 1902 by Chantiers et Ateliers de Saint Nazaire at Rouen for Compagnie de Navigation Française of Nantes, *Amiral Cécille* was an excellent example of the effect of the *prime* in encouraging the building of hulls with a long-superstructure. Her forecastle was 49-feet long, and her poop was 136-feet, extended by 44 feet by a flying bridge. Her superstructure thus occupied 229 of her total length of 282 feet. *Amiral Cécille* was destroyed by fire on 22nd January 1925 while laid up in the Canal de la Martinière. *[Author's collection]*

of Gustav Erikson's grain ships were of this rig. Basil Greenhill, writing in 'Sail's Last Century' (page 89), says 'This was…the era in which the standard big…merchant sailing vessels became the steel four-masted barque…'. Yet an analysis of the launchings from British yards from 1890 onwards shows that, of 571 vessels sent afloat, 34.2 per cent were three-masted barques compared with 32.3 per cent four-masted barques. More surprisingly, for anyone believing that the full-rigged ship began to go out of favour from the 1880s onwards in comparison with the barque with its lower manning requirements and equal – or better – performance, 25.6 per cent of the British vessels launched from 1890 onwards were full riggers, including four of the seven vessels built in 1903. Of the 225 French deep-water bounty ships built during the decade of the 1893 law, 68.8 per cent were three-masted barques and 16.8 per cent full riggers, compared with only 13.7 per cent four-masted barques.

'Hobart for orders'
The mileage component of the bounty system meant that vessels often took the longest route from port to port and made out-of-the-way calls before they reached their destination. Hobart,

Built in the last year of the 1893 bounty law was *Socoa* of Bayonne completed in 1902 by Chantiers et Ateliers de Saint Nazaire, and is seen loading cement for San Francisco at Stettin in 1906. Note how the line of the painted ports follows the topmost strake, a feature which distinguishes French sailing ships from their British counterparts, whose ports were typically one strake lower. *Socoa* was owned at the time by Société Bayonnaise de Navigation. Sold in 1907 and subsequently renamed *Thiers,* she was broken up late in 1927. *[Jurgen Meyer/Author's collection]*

Tasmania, became notorious in this respect. Vessels sailing from Europe for California, Puget Sound and the West Coast of South America, instead of thrashing westwards round the Horn, would go east-about via the Cape of Good Hope, taking advantage of the Roaring Forties and calling at Hobart for stores and orders. A vessel carrying case-oil from New York to Japan, or heading for New Caledonia for nickel ore, would load a token part-cargo for Tasmania as a pretext for calling there and to justify the bounty. The 14,000-mile passage, even in ballast, could be more than reimbursed by the mileage subsidy. Tasmania was conveniently situated for this purpose and the wide estuary of the Derwent River provided a cheap and secure anchorage. In 1908 27 French sailing ships called at Hobart. Other diversions might include Japan or the Dutch East Indies en route to the west coast of North America.

The bounty and profitability
The *prime* made a significant contribution to the financial viability of France's deep-water sailing fleet: the longer the voyages, the greater the profits. Some vessels made extraordinary returns annually or over a single voyage, compared with their British counterparts, struggling to make ends meet. The barque *Marguerite Molinos*, in her first year of work October 1897 to November 1898, covered 47 per cent of her building costs for her owners, the Société des

Asnières entering the Derwent River, Hobart, a port notorious amongst critics of the bounty ships. Built for the Société des Longs Courriers Français by Forges et Chantiers de la Méditerranée at Graville in 1902, she has a foremast planted almost in the centre of her long forecastle, whilst her poop stretches well forward of her mizzen mast. The 3,103 gross ton barque was sold in 1916 to Société Générale d'Armement, Nantes, but was captured and sunk by the raider *Möwe* in the Atlantic on 2nd January 1917 whilst on a voyage from Bahia Blanca to Pauillac with wheat. *[Author's collection]*

Voiliers Français of Le Havre, with a navigation bounty of 119,028 francs being added to her net freight earnings of 125,202 francs. In the same year the barque *Reine Blanche*, owned by Guillon et Fleury, also of Le Havre, made a profit of 33.19 per cent over a period of six months and five days, on a voyage Newcastle-upon-Tyne – Swansea – San Francisco – New Caledonia – Le Havre, with a navigation subsidy of 133,481 francs being added to freight earnings of 237,642 francs.

Among other profitable single-voyage earners of the turn of the century one may quote the *Charles Gounod* (25.6 per cent profit), *Général de Charette* (25.9 per cent), *Général Neumayer* (21.5 per cent) and *Général de Boisdeffre* (19.25 per cent). D'Orbigny et Faustin of La Rochelle, owners of the four-masted barque *Europe*, voyaged from Hamburg to Portland (Oregon) via Hobart in ballast, and then brought her one cargo, grain, from Portland to Ipswich.

Some of a ship's biggest profits would, of course, be made in the first years of her bounty qualification before payments began to decline. Critics used these earnings to attack the system but ship owners, naturally, pointed to them to attract investors.

The case for the bounty

The bounty system caused considerable resentment among ship owners of other countries who saw themselves injured by French protectionism, especially as trading conditions for sailing vessels worsened and sail fought a losing battle against steam. Resentment essentially focused on freight rates, which were critical in influencing sailing ship building and operation. The *prime* acted as a cushion against low rates and enabled French owners to ride out slumps and fluctuations in a way that British owners, for instance, could not. The bounty ships were able to accept freight rates which for others would be ruinous while at the same time sailing half way round the world in the ballast passages which were becoming more and more the rule for sailing ships. It may be that this unfair competition was a factor in persuading British owners to abandon sail, after trying unsuccessfully to agree minimum international freight rates for sail cargoes. On 10-11th December 1903 a sailing ship owners International Union was set up in Paris, with five British, three German and

three French representatives, with the aim of securing the sector's future by setting minimum rates below which charters would not be accepted. The Union met again in Glasgow in 1906 but all efforts proved unsuccessful in curbing the French advantage.

Strongly-voiced criticisms came from within France as well, from the moment the 1893 law was passed. Protests appeared in the press, from businessmen representing domestic interests such as land transport companies who could not see why they also were not given similar assistance, and especially from politicians in the National Assembly who denounced as a scandal the detours of thousands of miles (in order to deliver a few tons of goods to Hobart, for instance) whose real objective was to prolong the refundable route. In 1901 the Minister of Finance, Joseph Caillaux, said to the Chamber of Deputies: 'There have been built, under the influence of the 1893 law, sailing ships which have no other object than to circulate across the seas, in zigzag, no matter where, without cargo, sailing in ballast, with the sole aim of picking up the *prime*. They are costing the state dear'. A Deputy from

an inland constituency commented 'you are subsidising the stage coach at the expense of the railway train'.

Defenders of the bounty system included shipbuilders and ship owners, naval architects and marine engineers, and senators of coastal *départments*. The official thinking behind the *prime* (which, it must be remembered, benefited steam as well as sail) was that it supported the French shipbuilding industry; that a healthy merchant fleet was an adjunct to the navy in the training of seamen and the creation of a naval reserve; that it was thus vital for national defence and prosperity and the protection of the colonies; and that it promoted French overseas trade. Other arguments deployed were that part of the bounty was recovered by the state anyway, in the form of deductions, levies, duties and taxes; and that state disbursements were repaid by the earnings and savings made by not having to employ foreign shipping.

Shipbuilders claimed that the bounty was justifiable recompense for the exhorbitant French customs duties on imported raw materials, which gave cost advantages to British builders. An example cited was the offer by the

The highly profitable *Général de Charette* was built in 1898 by Ateliers et Chantiers de la Loire at Nantes for local owner Léon Guillon. The barque foundered on 3rd September 1900 after striking Ship's Rock in Le Maire Strait, whilst on a voyage from Swansea to San Francisco with coal. *[Author's collection]*

Clyde shipbuilder Archibald Macmillan in 1898-9 to construct a 3,150 ton deadweight sailing vessel for £15,000 (375,000 francs) while the same ship built in France would cost 600,000 francs – a 1.8 times advantage to the foreigner. The *prime* attracted private capital into shipbuilding, including the setting up of many new firms, saving yards and their associated industries from ruin and increasing shipbuilding employment to 20,000 workers.

Ship owners and their spokesman, the president of the Union des Armateurs de France (the Shipowners' Union of France), asserted that without the bounty they would not be able to operate, burdened as they were by customs and fiscal charges which their foreign rivals did not have to bear. The French merchant marine was prevented from competing on level ground, additionally, by for instance, the obligation under the bounty law for a vessel to touch at a French port before the legal year expired (which for a sailing ship sometimes meant an expensive tow at the end of a voyage), by the higher cost of repairs in France and especially by the expenses implicit in the regulations laid upon ship owners by the *inscription maritime*. Another argument deployed was that competition by the bounty ships lowered international freight rates and thus benefited French farmers to the tune of 15 million francs per year in the lower costs of imported guano and nitrates.

The overall sentiment, then, was that the French merchant marine was thus compensated for the greater costs it had to bear. The state was unwilling to renounce the financial benefits it received from ship owners, since this would have involved modifying rules and regulations, changing attitudes and perhaps losing jobs. It was only fair, therefore, for the state to give with one hand what it was taking away with the other.

French seamen and the *inscription maritime*

One of the arguments used by French owners to justify the bounty system was that the high cost of using French crews placed them at a commercial disadvantage. All French seamen were naval reservists up to the age of fifty, and enjoyed rights and working conditions not available to other nationalities. French merchant vessels were obliged to carry exclusively French crews, unlike the haphazardly recruited, polyglot crews of British, United States and Scandinavian vessels.

French seamen could not be discharged without good reason or compensation, or have their pay distrained. They received a three-month advance on joining, and the owners were responsible for repatriating them if the final discharge port was far from their home, or the ship was lost. Supervision of the ships' crews abroad was by French consuls, who would not allow a master to make up his crew with foreigners if French seamen were available. Seamen enjoyed what was, for the time, a generous scale of provisions and alcohol, similar to that in the French navy, and after 25 years of service were eligible for a pension when they reached 50. They also enjoyed medical supervision, hospitalisation, insurance and workmen's compensation schemes.

France did not have an indenture/apprenticeship system to train its officers, but selected men from the forecastle on merit and ability, so that every seaman had the possibility of achieving command. All this meant French seamen had a real stake in their profession, compared with the complete insecurity of most of those on British vessels.

Crews were mostly from Brittany, Normandy or the Vendée. One peculiarity of the French system was that the crews were not allowed shore leave at most ports, meaning that crews were very self-contained and did not readily mix with sailors from other nations. They had little reason to sail on ships on other flags, and indeed could do so only with authorisation.

A consequence of the pay and conditions they enjoyed, and the absence of shore leave, was that rates of desertion from French ships were about one sixth of those from British ships. But it did happen: in 1906, 17 of the 35-man crew of *Général Faidherbe* deserted in San Francisco. Captain Yves Menguy found them and brought them back on board at gunpoint.

The end of the bounty-ship boom

Deep-water square-rigger construction came to an end in France even more abruptly than in the United Kingdom. The expiry of the controversial law of 1893 at the end of 1902 was anticipated by new legislation on 7th April 1902 which stipulated that the 1893 law's subsidies would only apply to vessels laid down before 1st May 1902 and completed by 31st January 1903, and

The *Général Faidherbe* was built in 1901 were Ateliers et Chantiers de la Loire, Nantes for local Compagnie Maritime Française. She changed hands several times, to Société Nouvelle d'Armement in 1914, and to Société Générale d'Armement, also of Nantes, in 1917. She became one of the last bounty ships to bring grain home from San Francisco in immediate post-war years The 2,326 gross ton barque was broken up late in 1927. *[Author's collection]*

that no more than 45,000 gross tons of building could be commenced between 1st January and 1st May 1902. This third bounty law effectively ended the construction of large sailing vessels in France. The last square rigger built under the 1893 provisions was the barque *Rochambeau*, launched at Nantes by Constructions Navales in December 1902 for the Compagnie de Navigation Française of that city.

Coming into operation in 1903, the 1902 law placed a ceiling on the eligible tonnage which could be built each year, the total tonnage that could qualify for subsidy and, more importantly as regards sailing ships, changed the computation of the mileage bounty. The *prime* remained at 1.70 francs per gross ton for vessels under 600 tons; above that size the bounty decreased by 10 cents per 100 tons: and it was capped at 1,000 tons so that a 1,000-ton vessel only received 1.30 francs per ton and vessels larger than 1,000 tons were treated only as 1,000-tonners. To counter the charge that under the 1893 law a vessel could sail round the world in ballast and still make a profit, the new law stipulated that the bounty was not payable unless a cargo equivalent to at least two-thirds of the gross tonnage was carried for at least two-fifths of the distance sailed from departure from a French port until return to France. Although a vessel could still spend three-fifths of her voyage in ballast, the 1902 law effectively withdrew the bounty from deep-water sailing ships, favouring instead the construction of steamers and small sailing vessels of up to 1,000 tons. Only one sailing ship was constructed under this law, the 793-ton barquentine *Antoinette* – found to be too small for the Cape Horn trades and too big for the West Indies trade – and no more deep-water commercial square riggers were built in France (except for *France II*).

A ship owners' compensation scheme was introduced in the form of a payment of five centimes per day during the construction of a vessel up to 2,000 gross tons; four centimes up to 3,000 tons; and two centimes for vessels of 4,000 to 7,000 tons. Not surprisingly, this scheme was no stimulus at all and further legislation had to be passed on 19th April 1903, increasing the rates and endeavouring to prevent the sale abroad of virtually new vessels built under the 1893 law, and the disappearance of the French sailing fleet. As so often in the history of French maritime legislation, the scheme proved inoperable since it was immediately overtaken by new expenses and charges upon owners.

The bounty fleet on the eve of the First World War

Bounty payments for ships built under the 1893 law ran out in 1910, but fortunately higher freight rates prevailed in the period up to 1914 and the impact of the bounty could still then be seen in the huge size of those French sailing ship

A late and short-lived bounty ship was the big *Adolphe,* completed for Bordes in May 1902 by local builder Ateliers et Chantiers de France. The 3,245 gross ton, four-masted barque was wrecked on 30th September 1904 on Oyster Bank, New South Wales at the very end of a ballast voyage from Antwerp. *[Author's collection]*

The barque *Rochambeau* was the last square rigger built under the 1893 bounty act, launched in December 1902 at Nantes by Constructions Navales for the Compagnie de Navigation Française of that city. Sold to Société Anonyme des Voiliers Nantais in 1904, the 2,759 gross ton *Rochambeau* was wrecked on 30th August 1911 off Noumea towards the end of a voyage from Glasgow to Tchio with coal and coke. *[J. and M. Clarkson collection]*

companies surviving. These included the two biggest companies in the world. The best known – Antoine-Dominique Bordes of Dunkirk – still owned 45 big square riggers totalling 112,531 gross tons in 1914, but larger still was the Société Générale d'Armement of Nantes, with 52 ships grossing 119,704 tons. The Société Générale (formerly the Compagnie de Navigation Française) had built up its fleet in the decade prior to the war by taking over the vessels of companies in difficulties, such as Guillon and the Compagnie Maritime Française. At the outbreak of war the United Kingdom had around one million tons of sailing vessels, followed by France with over 600,000 tons and Germany with some 500,000 tons. The French fleet still included 112 big square riggers built under the bounty system, and there were still 140 bounty ships flying the *tricolore*. At the outbreak of the First World War A.-D. Bordes et Fils of Dunkerque had 46 square riggers of around 163,000 deadweight tons.

To be concluded.

The culmination of hull design for the bounty-earning vessel was the continuous spar deck, as in the *Joliette* of 1903, built by Forges et Chantiers de la Méditerranée, La Seyne. The 2,698 gross ton, three-masted barque had but a short career with Société Marseillaise de Voiliers. She was wrecked during a cyclone on 11th February 1909 while loading nickel ore at Tchio, New Caledonia for Le Havre. Relatively few ships with such a continuous upper deck, or spar deck, were built, as some harbour authorities considered that they should pay increased dues. [Author's collection]

Madeleine was a full-rigged ship with a long poop completed in November 1902 by Chantiers et Ateliers de Saint Nazaire for Société de Navigation du Sud-Ouest of Bordeaux. She was acquired by Bordes in 1904: note their trademark painted ports.

Madeleine was yet another victim of unrestricted submarine warfare. On 31st July 1917 she was about 200 miles south east of Santa Maria in the Azores on a ballast voyage from Bordeaux to Sydney when she was shelled and sunk by *U 155*. [Author's collection]

Of all the colonial powers which exploited Africa none were more rapacious than Belgium. The Congo was the nineteenth century creation of two energetic men, King Leopold (1835-1909) and Henry Moreton Stanley (1841-1904), neither of whom were Belgian. The king was of German origin and Stanley an American. Belgium was a country only 34-years-old when Leopold ascended the throne in 1865: history widely records him as vain, greedy, and overpoweringly ambitious. Using Stanley's explorative travels and knowledge, Leopold created by far the largest and most opulent private domain ever known: it was the size of western Europe. With a portfolio of treaties which Stanley had signed with various native chiefs, the infamous Berlin Conference (1884-1885) made one of the most astonishing decisions in history – it created the Congo Free State, not as part of Belgium, but as Leopold's personal estate, and so it remained until 1908.

With Stanley as his 'agent' Leopold's rule is recorded as being 'mercilessly exploitive' and it made him one of the richest men in the late nineteenth century world. Initially the fortune was based on rubber and ivory but mined materials soon followed. The management of the regime in the anything but 'Free State' of the Congo grew steadily more voracious and insatiable with its colonists practising nothing less than genocide on the African population. Such was the effectiveness of this process that a population estimated at 20 million in 1900 had shrunk to 12 million by 1950. The numerous atrocities recorded in the early 1900s led to widespread international protests and to the territory being 'gifted' to the Belgian state. If some Belgians citizens were at first reluctant to accept what much of the world saw as a blood-stained present, the Belgian-French corporations already there did not. Société Générale and its associate Union Miniere – created in 1904 – thrived by exploiting the mineral wealth of Katanga, producing cobalt, silver, zinc and - perhaps most vitally of all for world history by 1945 - uranium from which plutonium is refined, and without which no atomic bomb would have been made.

The River Congo remains the country's economic artery which, with its tributaries, provides 8,750 miles of navigable waterways. The Congo, the sixth longest river in the world, has two main barriers, the Boyoma Falls at Kisangani (formerly Stanleyville) and between Kinshasa (Leopoldville) the capital, and Matadi, the country's only deep water port, between which the river drops 850 feet, over 32 cataracts in 200 miles. As recently as 1957 there were no main roads between the capital and the state's two main cities, Kisangani and Lumumbashi (Elisabethville) in Katanga 800 miles to the south east. Rail links, on three different gauges, and a fleet of river vessels were the key to developing colonial Congo.

Asked by a United States author in 1953 who runs the country, the Belgian Governor General responded, 'I do'. At that time such was the international political pressure on Brussels that only seven years later in 1960 there was a precipitous granting of independence to the indigenous Congolese for which very little preparation had been made:

there were just two qualified African doctors. Belgium all but abandoned the diverse land that had given it so much wealth. There followed twenty years of civil wars, threats of Katanga seceding and a succession of local despots raping the wealth of the country; Joseph Conrad's 'Heart of Darkness' had become all too true.

Beginning of CBMC
Back in the 1880s Leopold's new domain needed an assured shipping link to 'the Mother Country'. Boma at the mouth of the Congo served as the main entry port until the up-river port of Matadi, on the south bank, opened on 20th June 1889. Here cargo could be discharged alongside and carried forward by the newly-opened rail link to Leopoldville. The dominance of the Elder, Dempster Line of Liverpool and its subsidiaries, the creations of Alfred Jones (1845-1909, knighted in 1901), ensured that one of their ships was the first into the new port. The British colonies in West Africa were extensively served by Elder Dempster. Jones had the ships and Leopold needed regular sailings for his Belgian staff (none of them settlers), for the cargo to develop his estate, and to carry away its produce. With a keenly developed political sense, Jones formed an alliance with Adolph Woermann of Hamburg and, with King Leopold's full approval, rationalised monthly sailings between Antwerp and Matadi, starting in 1891. An abrasive meeting between Leopold and Jones concluded with an agreement to form Compagnie Belge Maritime du Congo (CBMC) in January 1895: the totality of control by Elder, Dempster was emphasised by their ownership of 4,150 out of the 4,200 issued shares. At the same time Woermann set up a Belgian flag operation, Société Maritime du Congo, but despite (or perhaps because of) his placing two new buildings on its service, it made heavy losses and was discontinued in 1901. The two companies continued to have an operational agreement under the freight conference system but a new and detailed contract with the Congo State of 1898 restricted calls at other West African ports and this is also cited as a reason for Woermann's exit. There is also plenty of evidence that King Leopold mischievously played off one company against the other: this was in spite of Jones, as the Congo's Consul General in Liverpool, defending Leopold's human rights' record. Jones' position in this was made much more embarrassing because two of the most strident of Leopold's critics, Roger Casement and E.D. Morel, had at one time been employees of Elder, Dempster. Although CBMC's earnings were satisfactory, the investment by Elder, Dempster was disproportionate, and such was the division of profits that Elder, Dempster received only a modest return.

In 1895 CBMC inaugurated a service from its base port of Antwerp with *Leopoldville* (3,363/1895), and a year later she was joined by the *Albertville* (3,953/1896). From the start of operations until cargo-only ships joined the fleet in 1919, it was company policy to operate only passenger ships which also had cargo space. The operational control that Elder, Dempster exercised can be seen in the number of passenger-cargo ships that went from 'the Mother

CBMC's first *Albertville* of 1896 became Elder, Dempster's *Jebba* in 1898 (top). Homeward bound from West Africa for Plymouth and Liverpool, *Jebba* was wrecked at Bolt Tail, South Devon on 18th March 1907, as seen in the middle photograph. [Both: J. and M. Clarkson collection]

The *Leopoldville* of 1904 became Elder, Dempster's *Landana* in 1908, as seen here. She was soon sold, and as the Spanish *C de Eizagusrae* was mined with heavy loss of life on 25th May 1917. [J. and M. Clarkson]

Company' to CBMC and back again. The frequency was such that, between 1895 and 1909, 12 ships were involved, none of them staying on the Belgian registry for longer than five years. To the confusion of historians there were no fewer than four *Leopoldville*s, three *Albertville*s and three *Bruxellesville*s. The *Stanleyville* (1) (4,051/1900) was not returned to Elder, Dempster for she was wrecked off Axim, Gold Coast in May 1902. The *Albertville* (3) (4,793/1906) had been ordered as Elder Dempster's *Fulani* (2), transferred before completion to CBMC and returned to become *Elmina* in 1910; there were several similar transfers. These inter-fleet transfers did not require changes in the ships' colour schemes other than the hulls: CBMC's were light grey, a scheme which Elder, Dempster's passenger ships did not adopt until the 1930s.

The sudden death of Sir Alfred Jones in 1909 resulted, with almost indecent haste, in William Pirrie (1847-1924) and Owen Philipps (1863-1937, later Viscount Kylsant) taking over Elder, Dempster and incorporating it into the ever-growing Royal Mail group. Always attuned to local politics and sensibilities, Philipps ensured that the *Albertville* (4) was the first of a long list of ships built for CBMC by the John Cockerill shipyard at Hoboken, upstream from Antwerp, in 1912-1913. Philipps did not succeed Jones as chairman of CBMC – he probably did not have time – but the Royal Mail influence could be seen in the new ships and even more so in two near sisters built by Alexander Stephens of Glasgow, the *Elizabethville* (1) and the *Anversville* (2), and the *Albertville* (4) built by John Cockerill. There were at last three ships that could be said to reflect the increasing sense of national pride in Belgium's own ships. It was under Albert Thys that CBMC began to acquire a more Belgian character. Declining the chairmanship of the company, he was able to strike a deal with Elder, Dempster to sell 80% of their shares: the new shape of CBMC was 60% Bank d'Outremer, 20% Elder, Dempster/Royal Mail group, 20% three German shipping companies.

The adoption of a new company structure coincided with the signing of a revised contract with the Minister of the Colonies: more explicit and demanding than the previous rolling contract. There was to be a sailing from Antwerp every

Elder, Dempster's *Elmina* had been completed in 1906 as the third *Albertville* for CBMC. She was acquired and renamed *Elmina* in 1910, and sold in 1928. As *Iphigenia* and *Cairo City* she lasted until broken up at Blyth in 1949, but had seen little service during her last decade. *[B. and A. Feilden/J. and M. Clarkson]*

Elisabethville (1) of 1910 was the first cargo-passenger ship ordered and completed for CBMC. *[National Maritime Museum]*

The First World War and after

The First World War commenced on 4th August 1914 when Germany invaded Belgium and violated the country's declared neutrality. Withdrawing from Antwerp, CBMC operated from offices in St. Mary Axe, London and operationally became part of Elder, Dempster. Conveniently, most of the Belgian Ministry of the Colonies was re-established in London at the same time. Under the aegis of the government-in-exile, in 1916 CBMC became the largest part of a new holding company of Belgian shipping interests entitled Lloyd Royal Belge. It was considered essential to keep the service to the Congo open and the British government was dissuaded from requisitioning the three almost-new passenger-cargo ships. In August 1914 the *Anversville* (2) was northbound with 100 passengers onboard and with 700 tons of ivory amongst its cargo, whilst the *Elisabethville* was southbound. The *Albertville* (4) remained in Antwerp but sailed for Port Talbot on 12th September 1914, just ahead of the Germans occupying Antwerp on 9th October. After months of indecision the three ships established regular sailings from Liverpool to the Congo but such was the congestion on Merseyside that the UK terminal port was moved to Hull with passengers handled at Falmouth. A fall-off in southbound cargo for the Congo was compensated for by the ships being used on Elder, Dempster's services to West African ports.

With the intensification of the German submarine campaign in 1917 the northbound *Elisabethville* was torpedoed off Belle Iles, western France on the 6th September having just landed some of her passengers at La Pallice. Sinking in 20 minutes although with only 16 lives lost, the ship took with her a consignment of 13,000 carats of diamonds.

The replacement for the *Elisabethville* was ordered as soon as possible from Cockerill and entered service in 1922: her construction and that of sister *Thysville* (1) being seriously delayed by shortages of basic materials. The second ship was named after Albert Thys, the managing director during a crucial period of CBMC's history, 1911-1915. The two ships were updated versions of the pre-war trio, of the same basic design and continuing with steam reciprocating engines and coal-fired boilers when most ships of that type and period were given turbines and were oil-fired. Now that it had four passenger ships, in November 1922 the company offered a sailing to the Congo every fortnight. The volume of northbound cargoes was growing quickly with the colony's annual exports totalling 40,000 tonnes of copper, 5,000 tonnes of copal (a type of timber resin used in French polish), 37,000 tonnes of palm

three weeks, the southbound voyage taking 19 days, 21 days northbound; whilst delays caused by seasonal low water levels at the mouth of the Congo were not acceptable. The contract insisted that high-ranking colonial officials were entitled to luxury-grade cabins at no extra cost, and mail was to be carried free. At this time Société Générale bought into 30% of an expanded capital issue and began what was to become their dominant role in controlling the company.

The trio of new ships carried passengers in three sharply defined classes. Baronial splendour was the keynote of the décor in first class. Unlike the British and Portuguese colonies adjoining the Belgian Congo, Belgium never encouraged white settlement, but from an early period wives and children commonly made up a proportion of the passengers. The ships were coal-fired and had steam reciprocating engines driving twin screws giving a service speed of 14 knots. The pace of development in what was Belgium's national line was modest compared with that commonplace even in individual British shipping companies. For instance, in 1911 British India Steam Navigation took delivery of seven of their 'E' class (each 5,100 grt) from four builders in just one year.

The second *Elisabethville* in the Scheldt at Antwerp (above: note the cathedral). She was completed in 1921 by John Cockerill at Hoboken. Comparison with the photograph on page 116 shows her accommodation has been extensively rebuilt. *[Roy Fenton collection]*

Thysville (1) as completed in 1922 (left) and after rebuilding (below). *[National Maritime Museum, William Schell]*

kernels, and 5,000 tonnes of palm oil. However, there was insufficient demand to sustain a fortnightly frequency and sailings reverted to three weekly after only six months.

Surplus to requirements, the *Albertville* (4) was sold in 1923 to Portugal's Companhia Nacional de Navegacao. The main reason for her sale was probably that, for four successive years between 1921 and 1924, CBMC had made a loss, although this was largely attributed to its cargo ships.

In the summer of 1928 King Albert I (1875-1934) and his queen Elisabeth sailed on the *Anversville* (2) for a state visit to the Congo. It was Albert's second visit. As a result of his visit as the heir apparent in 1909, there was action to reverse much of the misrule of his uncle, King Leopold II. Now, as King Albert I, he was not only popular, but also a pioneering environmentalist, setting up Africa's first national park at Virunga.

Increasing levels of trade in 1926 resulted in CBMC buying Elder Dempster's *Ekari* which, having been built as a cargo ship by John Brown, had been modified to carry 90 passengers in two-berth cabins in what had been numbers 1 and 2 'tween decks. Renamed *Stanleyville* (2) she must have been the slowest passenger ship of the early years of the twentieth century as, despite having steam turbines, her service speed was just 11.5 knots. After only three years in service *Stanleyville* (2) was laid up in 1930 and sold for scrap in 1932. In their enthusiasm to sustain and expand Belgium's merchant navy, Antwerp's ship owners had a habit of buying the wrong passenger ships. In 1920 a related company to CBMC, Lloyd Royal Belge, had bought British India's *Indarra* (9,735/1912). She had been built for their Australian subsidiary, Australasian United Steam Navigation, to trade between Sydney and Fremantle. She was not a success and became infamous for rolling her way across the Great Australian Bight, as well as for

the prodigious hunger for coal of her seven Scotch boilers when sustaining 16 knots. After strenuous service as a First World War troopship and then three UK to Australia round voyages on charter to Orient Line, *Indarra* was bought by Lloyd Royal Belge (UK) Ltd. for their trade to the east coast of South America. She was to be joined by a quartet of new buildings, two each from Scotts and Dennys. The *Indarra* was renamed *Pays de Ways*, which is just what she did not do, and in 1922 Lloyd Royal Belge cancelled the whole project. British India repossessed the ship and she was sold to Japan's Osaka Shosen Kaisha group in 1924.

The long standing problem of Elder, Dempster's West African trade was shared by CBMC. Southbound cargoes tended to be compact, valuable and attracted a remunerative freight rate, whereas northbound cargoes were mostly raw materials which occupied a large volume, and could only afford a low freight rate. To complement a growing cargo ship fleet, in 1926 CBMC ordered two passenger-cargo ships. The *Albertville* (5) came from Ateliers et Chantiers de la Loire, St. Nazaire and the *Leopoldville* (5) from John Cockerill. Their design was uninspired. During the same period – 1926 to 1927 – Harland and Wolff were building in Belfast the twin diesel-engined *Accra* (2) (9,337/1926) and the *Apapa* (2) (9,333/1927). For their pair CBMC had specified two British-built steam-reciprocating engines with six coal-fired, Scotch boilers. Their four-cylinder, quadruple-expansion engines were built by Hawthorn, Leslie in Newcastle-upon-Tyne and produced 8,500 IHP at 80 r.p.m to give a service speed of 16 knots, which was two knots faster than their Elder, Dempster contemporaries. One wonders whether the two Elder, Dempster directors on the CBMC board ever commented on this contrast of main engines.

Albertville of 1928, the fifth of the name, as built. [F.W. Hawks]

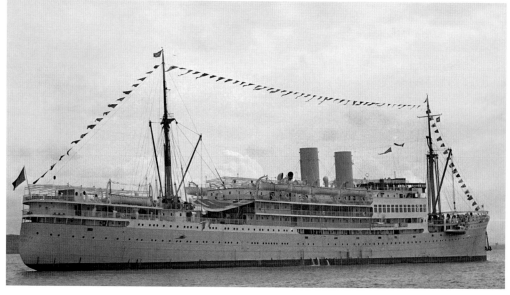

Two views of *Leopoldville* of 1929 in original condition in the River Mersey on 5th August 1934. The reason for her being dressed overall in the lower photograph is not known. [B. and A. Feilden/J. and M. Clarkson]

The two new 'Congo Boats', as they were known in Antwerp, emerged with two funnels (the after one a dummy) and accommodation for 358 passengers of whom 162 were in first class in single- or two-berth cabins. There were 162 in two- or four-berth cabins in second class. The crew totalled 232. Within the hull of 10,769 gross tons were four cargo holds and a large space forward of the engine room which could be used for either coal or oil fuel. Around 5,000 tonnes of cargo could be carried on a loaded draught of 25.4 feet. The layout of the first class accommodation was, for its time, spacious and airy with the whole of the 250-foot B Deck given over to four public rooms with two thirds of the area being open deck space. A fifth public room was a playroom for children which was an unusual feature for 1928: it was to be 23 years before Elder, Dempster had one built into a new mail boat. At the forward end of B Deck (on the centre castle) were eight suites each with their own bathrooms for 16 of those demanding, and presumably discerning, Belgian colonial civil servants.

What the CBMC directors would have known and provided for was that these new ships would soon be scheduled to call at a new port. For thirty years the Benguela Railway was being built for a thousand miles across the Bie Highlands in Angola from the natural harbour at Lobito (400 miles by sea south of Matadi) to Elizabethville in Katanga and onward into the copperbelt of Northern Rhodesia (now Zambia). Few railways were more vital to a developing area which commanded a global demand for its minerals. Through a British subsidiary the Benguela Railway was owned by Société Générale. The motive power of its trains was as spectacular as the route through which they hauled their freight: they were the wood-burning Beyer-Garretts, articulated locomotives with an all-up weight of 172 tonnes running on a three-and-a half-foot gauge track. When the entire length of the Bengeula Railway opened in 1931 the riches of Katanga no longer needed transporting by rail to East African ports as they had their own outlet at Lobito.

Merger

The quasi-nationally owned line, Lloyd Royal Belge, formed during the crisis of the First World War, had never been a financial success. In the early 1920s its fleet had grown to comprise 63 ships totalling 207,423 gross tons, amounting to 39% of the Belgian merchant fleet. In an era of much regulation on the carriage of cargoes on other than national flag ships, Lloyd Royal Belge had chosen to compete with larger and much longer established European shipping companies on some of the most commercially challenging of the world's trade routes – even to the Americas, North and South, and the Far East. The parlous state of Lloyd Royal Belge led to a merger of the company and CBMC to form Compagnie Maritime Belge (CMB) in February 1930. The integration of the two companies was a huge task, not assisted by the new board having 26 directors and being served by no fewer than 11 auditors. Société Générale were, as ever, very much an influential presence and it was their man Emile Francqui (1862-1935) who became the new chairman, and this was probably the cause of him dying in office, like Albert Thys before him.

It was the most inauspicious time for the new company to come on to the world's mercantile scene. The Great Depression which made many commodities almost worthless became ever deeper so there was no market for raw materials and no money to buy finished products. By 1934 the Belgian fleet was 20% smaller than it had been in 1920 and 40% of the remainder was laid up – 12 of them CMB ships, including *Stanleyville* (2). The two newest passenger ships were converted from coal-burning to oil-firing to save money and sailings from Antwerp to the Congo were reduced from one every 12 days to once every three weeks. *Leopoldville* (5) operated cruises in European waters but the losses continued, although at least the problems of the Kylsant crash that all but eliminated Elder, Dempster did not spread to CMB.

The hope offered by a conditional grant from the government in 1935 inspired CMB to consider the future shape of the much-expanded fleet and its liner trades. Three new cargo-passenger ships were ordered from Cockerill for the service to the east coast of South America, named after beach resorts in Brazil, Uruguay and Argentina. Concurrently modernisation was undertaken of the *Albertville* (5) and the *Leopoldville* (5) by making them faster by nearly two knots by re-shaping and lengthening their bows and installing Bauer-Wach exhaust turbines. Two 8,250 deadweight cargo ships each capable of carrying 1,100 tonnes of bulk palm oil were bought from Unilever off the stocks of a German yard; they were amongst a group of new buildings which where the only way Unilever could repatriate their profits from Nazi Germany. Most spectacular of all was an order to Cockerill to build a new passenger ship for the Antwerp-Lobito-Matadi route.

Fleet list

Official numbers given (where known) in the second line of each entry are Belgian.

1. ELISABETHVILLE (1) 1910-1917
7,017g 4,385n.
415.0 x 55.2 x 25.6 feet.
Q.8-cyl. (22, 31, 44 and 64 x 48 inches) by Alexander Stephen and Sons Ltd., Linthouse, Glasgow driving twin screws; 568 NHP, 14 knots.
1910: Laid down for Elder, Dempster and Co., Liverpool.
20.10.1910: Launched by Alexander Stephen and Sons Ltd., Linthouse, Glasgow (Yard No. 438) for Compagnie Belge Maritime du Congo, Antwerp, Belgium as ELISABETHVILLE.

12.1910: Delivered.
6.9.1917: Torpedoed and sunk by the German submarine UC 71, 17 miles east of Belle Iles, in position 47.05 north, 03.04 west whilst on a voyage from Matadi to Hull via Falmouth.

2. ANVERSVILLE (2) 1912-1938
7,745g 5,062n.
440.3 x 55.6 x 34.4 feet.
Q.8-cyl. (23, 33, 47 and 67 x 48 inches) by Alexander Stephen and Sons Ltd., Linthouse, Glasgow driving twin screw; 962 NHP, 14 knots.
30.5.1912: Launched by Alexander Stephen and Sons Ltd., Linthouse, Glasgow (Yard No. 450) for Compagnie Belge Maritime du Congo, Antwerp, Belgium as ANVERSVILLE.
8.1912: Delivered.

Anversville (2) of 1912 after her re-building. *[William Schell]*

5.10.1938: Arrived at Ghent to be broken up by Van Heyghen Frères.

3. ALBERTVILLE (4) 1912-1923
7,745g. 5,051n.
439.5 x 55.7 x 24.3 feet.
Q. 8-cyl. (23, 33, 47 and 67 x 48 inches) by Société Anonyme John Cockerill, Seraing, Belgium driving twin screws; 964 NHP, 14 knots.
12.1912: Delivered by Société Anonyme John Cockerill, Hoboken, Belgium (Yard No. 524) for Compagnie Belge Maritime du Congo, Antwerp, Belgium as ALBERTVILLE.
1923: Sold to Companhia Nacional de Navegação, Lisbon, Portugal and renamed ANGOLA.
1946: Renamed NOVA LISBOA.
1950: Sold to the British Iron and Steel Co. Ltd., and re-named BISCO 3 for delivery.
4.7.1950: Left Lisbon in tow of TURMOIL (1,136/1945).
7.1950: Broken up at Blyth by the Hughes Bolckow Shipbreaking Co. Ltd.

4. ELISABETHVILLE (2) 1921-1940
O.N. 200005 8,178g 5,172n.
439.1 x 57.0 x 34.1 feet.
Q. 8-cyl. (23, 33, 47 and 67 x 48 inches) by Société Anonyme John Cockerill, Seraing, Belgium driving twin screws; 964 NHP, 14 knots.

Albertville (4) of 1912 was sold to Portugal in 1923, and the top photograph shows her at Cape Town under the first name she took, *Angola*. It is dated January 1946, not long before her name was changed to *Nova Lisboa*. The middle photograph shows under this later name, again at Cape Town, in October 1949. She was broken up less than a year later. *[Both: A. Duncan/J. and M. Clarkson collection]*

Elisabethville (2) of 1921 as built (bottom). Compare this photograph with that of the rebuilt ship on page 112. *[National Maritime Museum collection]*

19.5.1921: Launched by Société Anonyme John Cockerill, Hoboken, Belgium (Yard No. 562) for Compagnie Belge Maritime du Congo, Antwerp, Belgium as ELISABETHVILLE.

11.1921: Delivered.

1930: Owners became Compagnie Maritime Belge (Lloyd Royal) S.A., Antwerp.

12.8.1940: Placed under the control of the Ministry of War Transport, London (Elder, Dempster Lines Ltd., Liverpool, and later Lamport and Holt Ltd., Liverpool, managers).

18.3.1947: Sold to the Ministry of Transport, London (Lamport and Holt Ltd., Liverpool, managers) and renamed EMPIRE BURE (O.N. 181651).

1949: Laid up in the Holy Loch.

1950: Sold to the Charlton Steam Shipping Co. Ltd. (Chandris (England) Ltd., managers), London and renamed CHARLTON STAR.

1958: Transferred to Maristrella Navegacion S.A., Panama (A.J. Chandris, Piraeus, Greece, manager) and renamed MARISTRELLA under the Liberian flag.

19.1.1960: Arrived at Osaka, Japan to be broken up.

12.2.1960: Demolition began by Iida Co. Ltd. at Sakai City.

5. THYSVILLE (1) 1922-1940
O.N. 35137 8,176g 5,171n.
439.1 x 57.0 x 34.1 feet.
Q. 8-cyl. (23, 33, 47 and 67 x 48 inches) by Société Anonyme John Cockerill, Seraing, Belgium driving twin screws; 964 NHP, 14 knots.

10.12.1921: Launched by Société Anonyme John Cockerill, Hoboken, Belgium (Yard No. 563) for Compagnie Belge Maritime du Congo S.A., Antwerp, Belgium as THYSVILLE

6.1922: Delivered.

1930: Owners became Compagnie Maritime Belge (Lloyd Royal) S.A., Antwerp.

15.10.1940: Under the control of the Ministry of War Transport, London (Lamport and Holt Ltd., Liverpool, managers).

13.5.1947: Sold to the Ministry of Transport, London (Lamport and Holt Ltd., Liverpool, managers).

5.2.1948: Registered in London as EMPIRE TEST (O.N. 181839).

19.6.1953: Arrived at Faslane to be broken up by Metal Industries Ltd.

21.1.1954: British registry closed.

6. STANLEYVILLE (2) 1926-1932
6,741g 4,090n.
405.2 x 54.2 x 32.9 feet.
Three steam turbines double-reduction geared to a single shaft by John Brown and Co. Ltd., Clydebank, Glasgow; 630 NHP, 2,500 BHP, 11.5 knots.

From 5th June to 11th October 1947, *Empire Bure* made two voyages from Liverpool to Matadi manned by Elder, Dempster personnel. This photograph is dated 13th June 1947. Note that she wears the funnel colours of managers Lamport and Holt Ltd. *[John McRoberts/J. and M. Clarkson]*

In this photograph, *Thysville* of 1922 has had her accommodation rebuilt along the same lines as *Elisabethville* (2). *[J. and M. Clarkson collection]*

Elder, Dempster's *Ekari* of 1920 seen here became *Stanleyville* (2) on transfer to CBMC in 1926. *[M. Cooper/J. and M. Clarkson]*

12.1.1920: Launched by John Brown and Co. Ltd., Clydebank, Glasgow (Yard No. 519c).

6.4.1920: Registered in the ownership of the African Steam Ship Co. (Elder, Dempster and Co. Ltd., managers), Liverpool as EKARI (O.N. 144502).

16.11.1926: British registry closed on acquisition by Compagnie Belge Maritime du Congo S.A., Antwerp, Belgium and renamed STANLEYVILLE.

1930: Owners became Compagnie Maritime Belge (Lloyd Royal) S.A., Antwerp.

1932: Sold to Hughes Bolckow Shipbreaking Co. Ltd., Blyth for breaking up but re-sold to Japanese breakers.

22.2.1933: Registered in Blyth under the ownership of Hughes Bolckow Shipbreaking Co. Ltd. for the delivery voyage.

8.6.1933: Arrived at Osaka.

4.7.1933: British registry closed.

7. ALBERTVILLE (5) 1928-1940
O.N. 13505 10,388g 6,063n.
1937: 11,047g 5,653n.
494.1 x 62.0 x 24.0 feet.
1937: 537.2 o.a., 521.8 b.p x 62.0 x 24.0 feet.
Q. 8-cyl. (29, 41, 59½ and 85 x 54 inches) by Hawthorn, Leslie and Co. Ltd., Newcastle-upon-Tyne driving twin screws; 1,326 NHP, 500 IHP, 15 knots.
1937: Low-pressure exhaust turbine fitted; 1,556 NHP, 16 knots.
1.1928: Completed by Ateliers et Chantiers de la Loire, St. Nazaire, France (Yard No. 260) for Compagnie Belge Maritime du Congo S.A., Antwerp, Belgium as ALBERTVILLE.
1930: Owners became Compagnie Maritime Belge (Lloyd Royal) S.A., Antwerp.
1936-1937: Rebuilt by the Mercantile Marine Engineering and Graving Dock Co. S.A., Antwerp.
11.6.1940: Bombed and sunk in Le Havre Roads whilst inbound from Bordeaux to evacuate British troops.

8. LEOPOLDVILLE (5) 1929-1944
O.N. 26691 11,256g 6,521n.
1937: 11,509g 6,941n.
478.8 x 62.2 x 35.0 feet.
1937: 501.8 x 62.2 x 35.0 feet.
Q. 8-cyl. (23^{13}/$_{16}$, 33^{7}/$_{8}$, 48^{7}/$_{16}$ and 68^{7}/$_{8}$ x 48^{7}/$_{16}$ inches) by Société Anonyme John Cockerill, Seraing, Belgium driving twin screws; 1,019 NHP, 15 knots.
1937: Low-pressure exhaust turbine fitted; 1,225 NHP, 16 knots.
26.9.1928: Launched by Société Anonyme John Cockerill, Hoboken, Belgium (Yard No. 623) for Compagnie Belge Maritime du Congo S.A., Antwerp, Belgium as LEOPOLDVILLE.
8.1929: Completed.
1930: Owners became Compagnie Maritime Belge (Lloyd Royal) S.A., Antwerp.

Albertville (5) is seen as built on 18th July 1934 (top). After completion of a rebuild in 1937, her appearance was modernised with a soft-nosed, raked bow and with her two stove-pipe funnels replaced by a single, well proportioned stack (middle). *[Both: J. and M. Clarkson collection]*

Leopoldville (5) as built on the Mersey on 5th August 1934. *[John McRoberts/J. and M. Clarkson]*

118

Leopoldville (5) after her rebuild in 1937. *[William Schell]*

1937: Rebuilt by the Mercantile Marine Engineering and Graving Dock Co. S.A., Antwerp.

19.9.1940: Placed under the control of the Ministry of War Transport, London (Lamport and Holt Ltd., Liverpool, managers).

24.12.1944: Torpedoed and sunk by the German submarine U 486 in position 49.45 north, 01.34 west whilst approaching Cherbourg in convoy on a voyage from Southampton with United States troops. There were 770 casualties.

9. **COPACABANA** 1938-1958
O.N. 72642 7,340g 4,350n.
459.8 o.l., 435.9 b.p. x 61.5 x 26.8 feet.
2SCDA 5-cyl. (24$^{7/16}$ x 55$^{1/8}$) Burmeister & Wain-type oil engine by Société Anonyme John Cockerill, Seraing, Belgium; 1,028 NHP, 14 knots.

19.10.1937: Launched by Société Anonyme John Cockerill, Hoboken, Belgium (Yard No. 654) for Compagnie Maritime Belge (Lloyd Royal) S.A., Antwerp, Belgium as COPACABANA.

5.1938: Delivered.

19.9.1940: Placed under the control of the Ministry of War Transport, London (Elder, Dempster Lines Ltd., Liverpool, managers) until 15.9.1945.

2.4.1958: Sold to VEB Deutsche Seereederei, Rostock, East Germany and renamed THEODORE KÖRNER.

1962: Sold to Altis Compania Naviera S.A., Famagusta, Cyprus (Troodos

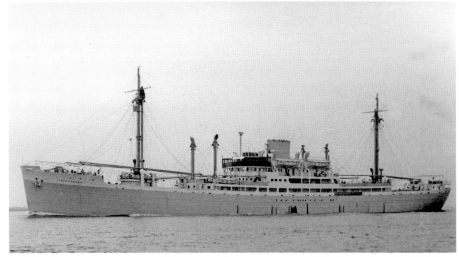

Two views of *Copacobana*, in wartime under Allied control (middle) and back with CMB post-war (bottom). *[J. and M. Clarkson collection; Roy Fenton collection]*

119

Copacabana as the East German *Theodor Körner* passing Gravesend whilst outward bound from London on 25th May 1967. *[Malcolm Cranfield]*

Both surviving 'Beaches' went to East Germany in 1958. *Mar del Plata* (above) became *Heinrich Heine* in 1958 (below, on the New Waterway in 1968). *[A. Duncan/Roy Fenton collection; Koos Riedijk/Malcolm Cranfield collection]*

Shipping and Trading (V. Hadji Ioannou), London, managers) and renamed NEDI II.
23.12.1972: Arrived Kaohsiung for breaking up by Nan Feng Steel and Enterprise Co. Ltd.

10. PIRIAPOLIS 1938-1940
O.N. 81476 7,344g 5,350n.
459.8 o.l., 435.9 b.p. x 61.5 x 26.8 feet.
2SCDA 5-cyl. (24^{7}/$_{16}$ x 55^{1}/$_{8}$) Burmeister & Wain-type oil engine by Société Anonyme John Cockerill, Seraing, Belgium; 1,028 NHP, 14 knots.
25.4.1938: Launched by Société Anonyme John Cockerill, Hoboken, Belgium (Yard No. 655) for Compagnie Maritime Belge (Lloyd Royal) S.A., Antwerp, Belgium as PIRIAPOLIS
7.1938: Delivered
11.6.1940: Bombed and sunk in Le Havre Roads.

11. MAR DEL PLATA 1938-1957
O.N. 78929 7,344g 4,350n.
459.8 o.l., 435.9 b.p. x 61.5 x 26.8 feet.
2SCDA 5-cyl. (24^{7}/$_{16}$ x 55^{1}/$_{8}$) Burmeister & Wain-type oil engine by Société Anonyme John Cockerill, Seraing, Belgium; 1,028 NHP, 14 knots.
1.7.1938: Launched by Société Anonyme John Cockerill, Hoboken, Belgium (Yard No. 656) for Compagnie Maritime Belge (Lloyd Royal) S.A., Antwerp, Belgium as MAR DEL PLATA.
17.9.1938: Delivered.
7.1940: Seized by Germany at Bordeaux having arrived from South America. Managed by Hamburg-Südamerikanischen D.G. for the Kriegsmarine.
9.8.1940: Designated transport for Operation 'Sëelowe', to carry 1,020 troops.
1944-45: Used in the Baltic to evacuate territories invaded by the USSR.
5.1945: Found at Aarhus with mine damage and returned to Compagnie Maritime Belge (Lloyd Royal) S.A., Antwerp.
26.3.1958: Sold to VEB Deutsche Seereederei, Rostock, East Germany and renamed HEINRICH HEINE.
1968: Sold to Loyna Compania Naviera S.A., Famagusta, Cyprus (Troodos Shipping and Trading (V. Hadji Ioannou), London, managers) and renamed CLEO II.
25.1.1973: Arrived at Kaohsiung for breaking up.

To be concluded.

PUTTING THE RECORD STRAIGHT

Letters, additions, amendments and photographs relating to features in any issues of 'Record' are welcomed. Letters may be lightly edited. Note that comments on multi-part articles are consolidated and included in the issue of 'Record' following the final part. Senders of e-mails are asked to provide their postal address.

Pole star

When I was junior officer in Blue Star during the fifties there came to us a relieving officer who was Polish, who had been third mate of the *Batory* (see 'Record' 53) and had jumped ship when she was in the Tyne for one of her post-war refits. Obtaining political asylum he anglicised his name to Leopold Allsford. To us juniors he was Uncle Leo and soon became a highly respected master.

Such was Leo's ebullience that he was known throughout the company as 'the magnetic pole'.
A.W. KINGHORN, 15 Kendal Avenue, Cullercoats, North Shields NE30 3AQ.

One for Mills and Boon?

I am sure Andrew Bell well knows that *Patani* (2) was launched by Scotts on 22nd April 1954 and not by Lithgows. How I can remember without checking is that for my second date with girlfriend, now wife, as an apprentice at Scotts I got a couple of passes to attend the launch. This was on a Saturday afternoon, postponed due to high winds the day before. Talk about an anorak!
JAMES POTTINGER, 1 Jesmond Circle, Bridge of Don, Aberdeen AB22 8WX

Brunshausen bits

I have been very interested in the articles in the past two issues on the Brunshausen reefers as I had hoped they would identify a very long outstanding mystery ship I photographed. On 10th March 1978, during my second-ever photographic expedition to Singapore, in the Eastern Anchorage I photographed under gloomy conditions the reefer *Frigo*, which was bunkering water and fuel. This name only appeared on the bow in rather rough paintwork and, due to the letter spacing, appeared to be possibly taken from existing letters of a previous name. The stern was blank of name and port of registry but she was flying the Singapore flag on the aft jackstaff. Unfortunately I did not get time to take the boat in closer for a check of any sign of former names. Funnel colours were dark blue with the conjoined capital letters HP in white.

I am sure this is one of the Brunshausen-class but as far as I have been able to ascertain this name has never appeared in any registers as such or the two instalments in 'Record'. Although I did notice in 'Record' 52, page 246, ship number 8 *Brunsholm* was reported as sold in 1978 to Singapore-registered owners and renamed *Pacific Fruit*. Not sure if there is possible connection there with *Frigo* being a temporary name?

This report of the *Frigo* may be of interest to the author who could possibly comment or advise any further information to explain this apparent mystery ship?
CHRIS GEE, PO Box 757, Fremantle, Western Australia 6959

In the last two photos of the Brunshausen reefer article ('Record' 52, page 248) both ships can be seen to have a number of large Yokohama fenders on deck. These are indispensable for high seas fish transfers or in exposed anchorages (equally useful in offshore oil also). In the North Pacific and Bering Sea I have frequently encountered such ships. Typically the fishing boat or a factory trawler is moored to windward of the packer and the fish transferred by union purchase-rigged derricks. In calm conditions the packer may well load port and starboard simultaneously.

Chris Gee's photo of the *Frigo*. Which Brunshausen reefer was she?

Banana boats were often quite tender (several photos show ships rolling); the motion of a tender ship being much easier on the delicate fruit than that of a stiff ship. I once watched a Russian banana boat departing Esmeraldas, Ecuador - cleared the river and altered course bringing swell on the beam - rolled heavily - that was a very tender ship.

In the Pacific Northwest there has been a joint-venture hake fishery for many years, Russia being the major recipient. Nowadays though the Canadian fishing boats catching the hake just transfer the trawl to the Russian factory ship for instant processing. There is also an agreed quota of fish landed and processed onshore.
JOHN ANDERSON, 523 Louise Road, Ladysmith, British Columbia, Canada V9G 1W7

More Union-Castle R class memories
Some of the southbound voyages on the fruit boats ('Record' 52) were in ballast, but often we loaded cement two bags high with cars on top - this was possible in the low-height 'tween decks. The cars were for Rhodesia as I believe only boxed vehicles could be imported to South Africa to protect their own car industry; the cement was often for Mauritius. Off season, we carried Army stores from London, Suez and Aden to East Africa; sugar from Mauritius to the United Kingdom; East African vegetable produce to Hull and Newcastle. These voyages were round the Cape both ways as the Suez Canal was closed. On the last of these voyages there were more bales of sisal from Tanga than space available. Charlie Lorrains had them stowed on deck and, when we called at Zanzibar for fresh water, a gang was ordered to stow them in the passenger accommodation on the boat deck (formerly the gunners' accommodation). They went in through the doorways but, when discharging in Hull, all the door frames were damaged as the bales got stuck on the door jambs and split them.

I did four voyages on *Rustenburg Castle*, dry-docking in Antwerp after the first when Captain Laurenson relieved Captain Hort. After a further two and a half voyages, he was transferred to the *Bloemfontein Castle* in Cape Town, when Captain Bidwell had to go to 'hospital'. I was one of the two cadets who transferred Laurenson's luggage. Bidwell had had the carpenter put shutters over his portholes so that the 'Germans couldn't see the lights'.

I have memories of doing a northbound mail run and had thought that it was on the *Roxburgh Castle* in mid-1955. From Peter Newall's book, I assumed that I was mistaken and it must have been the *Rustenburg Castle*. But I now realise that, since I did not join the *Rustenburg Castle* until August 1955, it cannot have been on that ship. So digging deep into my memory, I think that another mail boat, the *Stirling Castle* or the *Carnarvon Castle*, had a delay and could not sail on schedule from Cape Town. Although the delay was only a day or so, the mail contract required a sailing on schedule at 4pm on a Friday. So on the Friday morning a few mailbags, probably less than a dozen, were delivered on board. We sailed at the appropriate time and steamed like hell, although I am sure that we did not make the United Kingdom in 14 days. I suppose a penalty had to be paid. We anchored off Dover and the mail was off-loaded to a tender. We then continued on our way to the continental discharge ports. Has any one any comments on this memory?
MARC HANRECK, 44 Blake House, Porchester Mead, Beckenham, Kent BR3 1TN

South West scenes follow up
Terry Nelder has kindly pointed out that steam coaster in the middle photograph of Brixham on page 227 of 'Record' 52 is not, as the editor very tentatively suggested, the *Kilcoan* but the *Fordham* of 1897. Terry has a Salmon postcard of her in Brixham, posted in 1925, on which the name is clear. She was built as *Latchford* for owners in Cheshire and Lancashire, taking the name *Fordham* when sold to John Harrison Ltd. in 1915. Charles Waine has rightly suggested that she might be one of Harrison's ships, but his funnel colours, with a red band bordered with white on black are not those in the photograph. It is more likely that the letter 'H' on her funnel in Brixham is for Ernest Heinz, who managed *Fordham* on behalf of the London Transport Co. Ltd. from 1920 to 1926. After one other British owner, *Fordham* was sold to Antwerp owners as *Lola* early in 1929, but in October 1929 foundered off Selsey Bill whilst on a voyage from Porthoustock to London with a cargo of macadam.

'South West Scenes 1' touched briefly on the Exeter Ship Canal. By coincidence there is a very detailed, illustrated article by David Wheeler on the port of Exeter and the reason for its decline in 'Maritime South West No. 25', the 2012 edition of the annual journal of the South West Maritime History Society (published at 'The Holt', Exton, Exeter EX3 0PN).

Still in the South West, Terry Nelder has done some research into the tiny *Archmor*, shown at Truro on 7th July 1932 in 'Record' 53, page 20. His researches show this was not her only call at Truro. The Falmouth Harbour Log housed in the Bartlett Library reports her arriving for discharge at Truro on 7th December 1930. She came from Kinsale, presumably with grain. This was probably the cargo of *Archmor* when photographed in 1932, as she is alongside Trafalgar Wharf, and the premises of S. and L. Trounson, Corn and Flour Merchants.

The article on the small fleet of Gordon Sheves in 'Record' 53 did not include a photograph of the diminutive motor coaster *Archglen*, but Dave Hocquard has kindly supplied this image, taken by Peter Herbert at an unknown port. She carried this name only from May 1948 until her loss in October 1949.

Record 52 photos

Perhaps surprisingly, the caption to the bottom picture on page 229 of 'Record' 52 makes no side-mention of the ship alongside, with name *Burutu* clearly showing. She was one of a class of 13 war standard cargo vessels owned by Elder, Dempster, completed in 1918 as *War Swan* for the Shipping Controller, and bought by British and African in 1920. In 1930 she was laid up in the Dart until February 1934 when sold Greek. As *Demetrios Inglessis* she lasted until 1959 when broken up in Osaka. From her funnel, the next ship outboard might be a sister, but her markedly different cross trees do not encourage this conclusion.

Page 250 (right-hand middle photograph): surely that is the superstructure of *Pendennis Castle*, which was the latest mail liner in 1959? *Pretoria Castle* was not given a signal mast abaft the bridge until May 1965.
ROBERT LANGLOIS, Feu Follet, Maisons au Compte Road, Vale, Guernsey, GY3 5HF

Stockholm for certain

Yesterday I received my copy of 'Record' 53. As always, immediately I put the kettle on and make myself a brew so I can fully enjoy the contents. On page 28 appears this nice picture as the editor says a 'busy day in an unidentified port'. This drew my attention and, after some research in my collection, this picture has revealed her identity. It is without doubt Stockholm, in the background we see the *Strathnaver* (22,548/1931) and the date this picture was taken is 25th July 1935. I don't know why these ships are in port at this date, or is it just a coincidence?
BEN SCHOLTEN, Titus Brandsmastr. 131, 2286 RE, Reijswik, Netherlands

The well-dressed ship

I was especially interested in the explanation of the flag dressing of the *Riebeeck Castle* ('Record' 53, page 57). I cannot share David Wittridge's surprise at the number of flags available as my experience of British ships of the period was that they were never short of bunting. Despite the gradual disappearance of the need for multiple flag hoists, the normal suite consisted of two sets of the alphabet, numerals and substitutes. Of course this made for a pretty full flag locker on the bridge but it also offered the third mate, as custodian of the contents, several useful places for the concealment from customs rummagers of a bottle of spirits or a few round tins of fifty cigarettes.

No doubt at least one of your readers will come up with an authoritative account of dressing a ship overall. I would imagine that most ships would have found that the exercise severely taxed resources other than the flag complement. The textbook proposes the use of a messenger, to which the connected flags were attached, positioned via the replacement of the topmast dummy gantlines. Your photographic reproduction is so good that the photograph clearly shows this line coming down past the foremast truck. The *Riebeeck Castle* is relatively lightly rigged with tall topmasts and little top hamper. Imagine the exercise carried out on a ship with shorter topmasts, more superstructure and carrying an extensive deck cargo!

The changing architecture of ships of course made such flag dressing virtually impossible as topmasts became a thing of the past. The two photographs of the *Patani* on page 59 illustrate this nicely. That signal mast by the funnel in the lower picture shows that flag flying was limited to the extent that a courtesy ensign, a house flag and the normally mandatory 'H' and 'Q' flags would have occupied all the available halyards. So perhaps dressing overall was an exercise best left to the ships of the Grey Funnel Line and their large crews long familiar with such routines?
JOHN GOBLE, 55 Shanklin Road, Southampton SO15 7RG

Apologies

Two correspondents we omitted to thank in the last issue were Alan Phipps and David Salisbury: their corrections to previous editions were noted, but we did not acknowledge these gentlemen. To make matters worse, we did not even credit David for the photograph of *Dnestrovskiy Liman* on page 58. Grovelling apologies all round.

The almost new *Pendennis Castle* at Cape Town in January 1959. *[J. and M. Clarkson collection]*

RECORD REVIEWS

A CUMBERLAND ENDEAVOUR
Hine Bros. of Maryport: The People, The Ships and The Town
By Ian Hine
260 x 204mm softback of 142 pages
Published by Words by Design and
available from Ships in Focus at
£17.50.

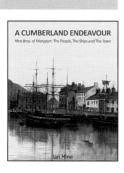

The Hine Brothers, Wilfred and Alfred, were by a large margin the most significant ship owners in the Cumberland town of Maryport. From 1868 to their company's rather precipitate demise in 1909, the brothers separately and in partnership owned over fifty deep-water and coastal sailing ships and steamers. These worked in a variety of trades, with sailing ships running to Australia, steamers working on the Holme Line service to North America, and coasters carrying iron ore and rails. As its subtitle indicates, Ian Hine's book is a rather homely account of his ancestors' family life, the fortunes (or more often misfortunes) of the Hines' ships and their masters, and the family's often important influence on the town's dock developments.

The author has relied heavily on research work done for him in local newspapers, and on family history. There are no details given of primary sources, just a list of books consulted, but it would appear from the text that letters from the ships' masters to Hine Brothers have survived. Along with passages from the local newspapers and from 'Sea Breezes', this correspondence is quoted extensively, and often provides vivid descriptions of casualties and of the difficulties of a ship master's life. The author writes fluently, although he is rather over-keen on exclamation marks, and makes some questionable generalisations about maritime matters. He interweaves abundant domestic details of the family with accounts of the ships' voyages, their casualties and their masters' careers (a welcome feature, as their captains tended to have long careers with Hine Brothers), and with the long and rather depressing story of the failure to fully develop Maryport's docks which eventually doomed the town as a port.

The intended audience for the book is evidently those with an interest in Maryport's past and the fortunes of its largest ship owner, and the book is very much in the tradition of providing undemanding local history. The author confines himself to relating what happened rather than asking, as a maritime historian might do, why Hine Brothers succeeded in operating in a variety of rather different trades, and why an apparently successful operation failed so precipitately in 1909.

It may be unfair to be too critical of such a book from a maritime history perspective, but the inclusion of a fleet list as an appendix brings the book firmly into shipping history territory. The list covers only the ships owned by the partnership of Wilfrid and Alfred Hines, not those in which they previously had individual interests. Detail is limited: for instance, owners prior to and after the Hines are not always given. Fates of the vessels are severely truncated, although for those lost whilst in Hines' ownership there are often exhaustive details elsewhere in the text, which makes it a pity that there is no index, not even of ships' names. Where

the fleet list section is most deficient, however, is in the accompanying illustrations. Whereas those elsewhere in the book are mostly acceptable, the illustrations accompanying the fleet list are reproduced to no more than cigarette card size. Even at this small size some are of pitifully low resolution, such as a well-known shot of the *Imperial Prince* of 1890 (later *Myrtle Holme*). Even worse, two photographs show the wrong ship. That purporting to be *Ardmore* built in 1872 and lost in 1899, is actually the Basil Feilden photograph of the *Ardmore* of 1921, owned by the Cork Steam Packet Company. At least these ships share a name, but the photograph which claims to show the 310-foot *Fern Holme* (1883 to 1888) is a post-Second World War view of much smaller steam coaster. None of the photographs are credited.

'A Cumberland Endeavour' is clearly the result of much work by the author and his researchers. It is welcome in shining some light on an intriguing ship owning partnership, but this reviewer would have preferred a more rigorous, questioning approach to writing the history of Hine Brothers.

Roy Fenton

FROM HIGH ARCTIC TO ANTARCTICA
Ships of Thom Companies on the Seven Seas
By Matti Pietikäinen
290 x 227mm hardback of 576 pages
Published by Thominvest Oy, Helsinki
and available from Ships in Focus at
£52.00.

Those writing the histories of shipping companies would love to know why decisions were taken, for instance to buy or sell a particular ship, or to enter or leave a particular trade. In this book the author can answer these questions because he worked for the owner in question, he knew those who took the decisions and can discuss their consequences, whether good or bad. The Thom companies wholly or part owned a number of ships between 1957 and 2007, under a variety of company names (Oy Thombrokers Ab probably being the best known, although this is relative) and joint ventures which are explained in detail in the first chapter. Although its total fleet was modest, the group was once rated Finland's sixth biggest ship owner, encompassing an interesting range of ship types, from a former heavy-lift vessel, through general cargo steamers and motor vessels, bulk carriers of various sizes, small specialised tankers, ro-ros, to deck cargo barges and a tug.

Author Matti Pietikäinen was manager of the group's maritime business from 1980 to 1994, and is also an experienced ship researcher and author, and has thus been able to compile a remarkably full history of each of the 18 wholly owned ships. Whilst concentrating particularly on their period under group ownership, he has also extensively researched careers under previous and subsequent owners and names, and gives a wealth of background. For instance, the first ship owned, *Make*, was once Christen Smith's *Beldis*, but had much of her heavy lift gear removed on her sale. The thirty pages devoted to *Make* includes a detailed account of how Christen Smith began and how he and Armstrong, Whitworth and Co. collaborated to make *Beldis* the first heavy lift ship. Her periods under other names are covered, not always in so much detail concerning the owner, but often to the level of voyages undertaken and repairs required. Illustrations of ships in various stages of their lives are copious and well reproduced. Each chapter is referenced. In addition to the text there is a detailed fleet list of thirty nine wholly or part-owned vessels. There are illustrations of the house flags used and of the surprising variety of funnels carried by the ships. The book is comprehensively indexed, and a subsidiary contents page lists the seventeen sections of text which deal with general aspects of Finland's shipping history between 1950 and 2000. The text is written

in English throughout, and generally very clear, although the explanations of some technical terms are a little opaque.

Make no mistake, this is big book, beautifully produced, and this is reflected in its price. But one would be hard pressed to name another book which gives such a detailed, intimate and honest history of a modern shipping company's life and times and those of its ships. It is worth every pound.

Roy Fenton

BOSUN'S LOCKER

Back to 'Record' 49

In 'Record' 49 we carried a photo of a tug assisting a liner (49/02) which in 'Record' 50 was identified by Tony Smyth as being the *Flying Falcon* of 1878. However, in 'Record' 51 Geoff Holmes threw his hat into the ring saying it was the *Enterprise* of 1885 and supplied a picture to back up his notes. Here I must add that I have a negative of the same print, which came from John McRoberts, marked up as being *Enterprise*. No further comments were received.

At a recent sale I picked up a page from an old album which bears the three very old sepia photographs reproduced below. Across the bottom of the page is scrawled *Knight of Malta* and the name can be read on the paddle box in

the larger photo (54/01c). In the margin there are pencilled notes: '*Knight of Malta*, originally *Speedwell*, built 1861 at Liverpool, 132 tons, Mersey Steam Tug Company.' There is also a note of the make up of the fleet: *Knight of Malta, Knight of the Cross, Knight of St John,* and *Knight of St Patrick*. In the 1892 'Mercantile Navy List' all are managed by J. Prendeville, Liverpool. Two tugs are illustrated: compare the funnel colours, the paddle box vents and the position of the wheelhouse in 54/01a and b and 54/01c. There is some indecipherable writing on the banner strung between the funnels and the mast in 54/01c. In view of the similarities between 49/02 and 54/01b comments are invited. And what of the tow in 54/01a: part of a landing stage?

54/01a

54/01b

54/01c

Photo 51/01

Bertil Palm writes from Trelleborg to put one of the editors out of his misery concerning this photograph of a steamer wrecked near Eastham. Her name is not *Canada* but *Canadia*, and at the time of her loss she was owned by Rederi A/B Svenska Lloyd of Gothenburg. On 23rd December 1919 she was on a voyage from Gothenburg to Manchester with wood and general cargo when she grounded outside the entrance to the Manchester Ship Canal after the line to her tug broke. At the next low tide she broke in two and was later condemned as a constructive total loss. The 1,558 gross ton *Canadia* was British-built, completed in 1882 by William Pickersgill and Son, Sunderland as *Longueil* for a single-ship company managed by Morel Brothers and Co., Cardiff. She was sold to Germany as *Albert Koppen* in 1897 moving to Sweden and the name *Canadia* in 1909. Svenska Lloyd bought her in 1916.

Photo 53/01

Tony Smith identifies the Norwegian ship on page 61 as the *Pollux* (1,676/1921), built by Helsingør Jernskibsverft & Maskinbyggeri as the Danish *Gulfaxe* and owned by Bergen Line from 1922 to 1948. She then became Egil Naesheim's *Vardal*, a frequent visitor to British ports. She finished her long career in the Far East, under the Philippines flag first as *Patriot* and finally as *San Augustin* before being broken up in 1981. A photograph of *Pollux* by Harry Stewart (top) confirms her identity, but shows her with 'proper' cross trees which are lacking in photograph 53/01. By the time she was photographed as *Vardal* (middle) her superstructure had been considerably rebuilt and she had an enclosed wheelhouse.

Photo 53/03

Dave Hocquard, David Rowe and Geoff Holmes (who supplied the photograph) agree that the small steamer in this photograph in the Mersey is the Isle of Man Steam Packet Company's *Douglas* (813/1889). Built and engined by Robert Napier of Glasgow, she was purchased from the London and South Western Railway Company in July 1901. She was formerly their *Dora* and was replaced in the railway fleet by *Vera* (1,136/1898). *Dora* then became a relief vessel until sold to the Manx company.

Pollux in Bergen Line colours (top) and in post-war condition as *Vardal* (middle). *[Harry Stewart/J. and M. Clarkson; Roy Fenton collection]*

For comparison a further view of *Douglas* and one where her name can be clearly read. *[J. and M.Clarkson collection]*

126

Douglas ran the winter and wartime mail services between Liverpool and Douglas 1901-1923 and in summer was used more generally on secondary and relieving services. In the autumn of 1909 she was reboilered and slightly modernised in an effort to get a better match for the Steam Packet's third *Snaefell*, then on order to improve the winter service. Her end came on the 16th August 1923 when she collided with the steamer *Artemisia* (5,739/1901) in the Mersey and sank in 20 minutes.

David Rowe notes that, given her length of service, there are surprisingly few good photographs of *Douglas*. One of the clearest is a Manx Museum shot reproduced on page 35 of Connery Chappell's 'Island Lifeline'. This shows the same pattern of centre castle portholes as in 53/03, the same cargo rig, the same prominent pair of ventilators behind the bridge, set to port and a single thin post right at the bow. Another photo from the port bow

on page 16 of John Shepherd's 'Life and Times of the Steam Packet' is our ship again, the main difference being that the black hull paintwork is carried a deck higher. Lastly, Duckworth and Langmuir's 'West Coast Steamers' has a view of her leaving Douglas harbour.

David is sure that *Douglas* could carry cattle and notes that it was the habit on the inward service to drop mails and passengers off at the Liverpool Landing Stage and then go up river to anchor in The Sloyne or unload cargo in Coburg Dock, before returning the next day to Douglas. On the occasion she was photographed, *Douglas* may also have been calling in over the water, as suggested, to unload cattle from the island, en route to anchorage or dock. The large chimneys in background (near the foremast) *could* be Clarence Dock Power Station in Liverpool. But David thinks there is something not quite right about the angle of the light as it hits the ship's ventilators on a sunny, misty day. He

can recall photographs showing factory chimneys just behind Woodside. So it is possible that *Douglas* is in fact swinging into the Princes Landing Stage from up river, with the light in the east, to pick up the morning sailing to Douglas.

54/02

We have been asked to identify the port in which *Sea Venture* and another steamer are berthed (below). It has the feel of a town in the south east of England. The gasholder and ornate church tower beyond give clues, as may the large building in the background at the extreme right (a brewery?). The legend on the wood warehouse simply reads 'Teak – Mahogany – Hardwood'. The photograph dates from the 1930s: the 2,327 ton *Sea Venture* was built by Swan, Hunter and Wigham Richardson Ltd. in 1930 for Dover Navigation Co. Ltd. and was sunk by *U 34* on 20th October 1939 during a voyage from the Tyne to Tromsø with coal.

54/02

Empire Lark

Roy's article on the British-flag Hog Islanders started me thinking about other groups of ships which appear to have had little, or nothing, written about them. Various groups came to mind and especially some relating to the last war. As regards new-built ships, the CAM-MAC ships (catapult armed merchantmen and merchant aircraft carriers) came to mind. The former was made up of 27 government-owned along with eight others taken up from private owners. The MAC ships were less numerous - only 19 in total - a mixture of tankers and dry cargo ships. Well documented, these two types would not be too hard to research and would make a

decent article with plenty of illustrations available. Perhaps too big for 'Record' but maybe the subject a small book. If someone would take on the writing I will be happy to sort out the illustrations. Thinking about older ships led me on to those captured during the Second World War and the ones confiscated from Germany and later allocated to the United Kingdom. These two groups contain many very interesting ships but again too many for a 'Record' article. The last lot considered were the ships loaded with surplus munitions, taken out to sea and sunk. An easy way of disposing of such material but a method which may come back to haunt us, or more likely, our children and grandchildren. How many ships were taken up for this I do not know. I have seen articles about them but which did not cover them in depth. Has anyone a definitive list of these vessels?

My musings led me to have a look what was tucked away in the old locker and I came up with just one relevant photograph, of the *Empire Lark* lying in Millbay Docks at Plymouth wearing her former owner's funnel colours. There was little information on the back of the picture other than the name of the ship, the place and the date - 30th December 1946.

Empire Lark was completed in Kiel, Germany in 1921 as the *Martha Hemsoth* for M. Sloman and Company of Hamburg. Driven by two steam turbines she had a gross tonnage of 4,949, was 407 feet in length and had a beam of 54 feet. In 1924 she was sold to Wilhelm Hemsoth A.G., also of Hamburg, without changing her name. 1926 saw her sold to Hanseatische Reederei A.G. (G.J.H. Siemers & Co.), Hamburg and renamed *Kersten Miles*. In 1937 she went to Hanseatische Reederei Emil Offen & Co., again of Hamburg. The *Kersten Miles,* on passage from Argentina to Germany with a cargo of wheat, arrived at Las Palmas, Canary Islands on 27th October 1939 with machinery damage and was interned, no doubt spending the rest of the war there. In 1945 she was surrendered to the United Kingdom in prize and placed under the management of Sir R. Ropner and Co. Ltd. by the Ministry of War Transport.

Reference to Mitchell and Sawyer's 'The Empire Ships' tells us that her loading of obsolete ammunition was not straightforward. Having been selected for scuttling, she left Plymouth in tow on 29th January 1947 for Barry in South Wales, arriving there on the 1st February. The loading of her full cargo of chemical warfare gas bombs and shells commenced on the 3rd.

However, early 1947 saw much severe weather, with ice and snow causing long delays in bringing the cargo alongside with the nature of the cargo causing further delays. The loading of 7,669 tons of ammunition, along with 20 tons of contaminated earth, was completed on 18th July 1947 and on 27th *Empire Lark* left Barry in tow of the Admiralty tug *Dexterous* escorted by a frigate. She was sunk in position 47.55 north, 08.25 west, roughly 200 miles south west of Lands End.

There is some doubt about the exact date on which the *Empire Lark* was sunk. One respected source gives her as sailing from Barry on the 27th and another claims that she was actually sunk on the 27th. Possible, but unlikely.

54/03. To complete this issue can anyone please tell us something about this photo? The ship is the *Cormorant* of Cardiff. Completed at Preston in 1878 she was originally registered at Scarborough. In 1903 *Cormorant* was re-registered at Cardiff in the ownership of William H. Tucker, Pierhead, Cardiff. Can anyone tell us anything about the event depicted and what became of her?